ETERNAL EMPIRE

THE OTTOMANS AT WAR

Written by Richard Bodley Scott, assisted
by Nik Gaukroger, James Hamilton,
Paul Robinson, Matt Haywood and
Xavier Codina

OSPREY
PUBLISHING

First published in Great Britain in 2008 by Osprey Publishing Ltd.

© 2008 Osprey Publishing Ltd and Slitherine Software UK Ltd.

Osprey Publishing, Midland House, West Way, Botley, Oxford OX2 0PH, UK
443 Park Avenue South, New York, NY 10016, USA
E-mail: info@ospreypublishing.com

Slitherine Software UK Ltd., The White Cottage, 8 West Hill Avenue, Epsom, KT 19 8LE, UK
E-mail: info@slitherine.co.uk

A CIP catalogue record for this book is available from the British Library

ISBN: 978 1 84603 401 5

Rules system written by Richard Bodley Scott, Simon Hall and Terry Shaw
Page layout and cover concept by Myriam Bell
Index by Glyn Sutcliffe
Typeset in Joanna Pro and Sleepy Hollow
Cover artwork by Peter Dennis
Photography by Jeremy Jenkins, Neil Hammond, Dan Hazelwood, Essex Miniatures
& Kingmaker Miniatures
Page design features supplied by istockphoto.com
All artwork and cartography © Osprey Publishing Ltd
Project management by JD McNeil and Osprey Team
Technical management by Iain McNeil
Originated by PDQ Media, UK
Printed in China through Worldprint Ltd

08 09 10 11 12   10 9 8 7 6 5 4 3 2 1

FOR A CATALOGUE OF ALL BOOKS PUBLISHED BY OSPREY MILITARY
AND AVIATION PLEASE CONTACT:

NORTH AMERICA
Osprey Direct, c/o Random House Distribution Center, 400 Hahn Road,
Westminster, MD 21157
E-mail: info@ospreydirect.com

ALL OTHER REGIONS
Osprey Direct UK, P.O. Box 140 Wellingborough, Northants, NN8 2FA, UK
E-mail: info@ospreydirect.co.uk

FOR DETAILS OF ALL GAMES PUBLISHED BY SLITHERINE SOFTWARE UK LTD
E-mail: info@slitherine.co.uk

Osprey Publishing is supporting the Woodland Trust, the UK's leading woodland conservation
charity, by funding the dedication of trees.

www.ospreypublishing.com
www.slitherine.com

CONTENTS

INTRODUCTION

This army guide covers the armies of the Ottoman Empire and its enemies and allies from 1299 to 1500 AD.

During this period the Ottoman state expanded from a tiny ghazi beylik in the north-west tip of Anatolia into a mighty empire occupying modern Turkey, Greece, Bulgaria, Serbia, Albania, Macedonia, Bosnia and parts of Romania. In the process it swallowed up the Anatolian emirates, the Byzantine Empire, the Latin states in Greece, the Bulgarian and Serbian Empires, Albania and Bosnia, and made vassals of the Principality of Wallachia and the Khanate of the Crimea. It also came into conflict with the Kingdoms of Hungary and Poland in the West and Timur (Tamerlane) and subsequently the White Sheep Turcomans in the East.

In a sense, the wars of Ottoman expansion in the West were a continuation of the Crusades, with the boot being on the other foot as the Christian states of south-eastern Europe were progressively invaded and conquered by the forces of Islam.

When Constantinople fell to the Turks in 1453, this ended 1,500 years of Roman Imperial history in the East and marked the final extinguishing of the Roman Empire, which had fallen in 476 AD in the West. Constantinople (modern Istanbul) became the capital of the young and aggressive Ottoman Empire, which continued to expand in the 16th century until it threatened the very existence of Christian Western Europe.

This period also saw the rise and fall of other states: the decline of the Tatar Golden Horde was matched by the amazing territorial expansion of the Grand Duchy of Lithuania and the expansion of the Great Principality of Moscow to rule most of the former Russian principalities, forming the basis of the modern state of Russia. The Ordensstaat of the Teutonic Knights in the Baltic reached its maximum expansion before being defeated and losing most of its territories.

These times also saw the first Protestant (Hussite) Reformation in Bohemia, and the first wars of religion between Catholics and Protestants – in which the Hussites, with their innovative use of battle wagons, were mostly successful.

From a wargaming point of view, the era offers a wide variety of diverse and colourful armies, and a wealth of interesting tactical challenges. Whether relying on horse archery, the mighty charge of lance armed knights, or defensive formations of infantry secured by field fortifications or battle wagons, the armies in this book will always be thought provoking and entertaining.

Ottoman Gazi and Turcoman horseman ambushed by a West Anatolian infantryman, by Angus McBride.
Taken from Men-at-Arms 140: Armies of the Ottoman Turks 1300–1774.

EARLY OTTOMAN TURKISH

With the decline of the Seljuk Sultanate of Rum and the Byzantine Empire in the later 13th century, Anatolia came to be divided between a number of effectively independent Turkish emirates. The most aggressive of these, in the far north-west, was ruled by Osman I (from whom the name Ottoman derives), son of Ertuğrul. From small beginnings, the Ottoman Beylik expanded rapidly at the expense of the Byzantines. In 1299 Osman Bey declared himself independent of the Seljuk sultanate.

As the closest Muslim state to the Christian lands, the Ottoman Beylik attracted large numbers of nomads, adventurers and fanatical ghazis, who formed the bulk of the army in the early years. However, c.1362, Osman's grandson Murad I created a new standing army of regular infantry, the Janissary corps – see the Later Ottoman Turkish list below.

This list covers Ottoman armies from the traditional date of the foundation of the Ottoman Empire by Osman I in 1299 AD, until the foundation of the Janissary corps by Murad I c.1362.

Timariot

EARLY OTTOMAN TURKISH STARTER ARMY		
Commander-in-Chief	1	Field Commander
Sub-commanders	2	2 x Troop Commander
Timariots	2 BGs	Each comprising 4 bases of timariots: Superior, Armoured, Undrilled Cavalry – Bow, Swordsmen
Ghazis	2 BGs	Each comprising 4 bases of ghazis: Superior, Protected, Undrilled Cavalry – Bow, Swordsmen
Ghazis	3 BGs	Each comprising 4 bases of ghazis: Superior, Unprotected, Undrilled Light Horse – Bow, Swordsmen
Azabs	2 BGs	Each comprising 8 bases of azabs: Average, Unprotected, Undrilled Light Foot – Bow
Camp	1	Unfortified camp
Total	9 BGs	Camp, 28 mounted bases, 16 foot bases, 3 commanders

BUILDING A CUSTOMISED LIST USING OUR ARMY POINTS

Choose an army based on the maxima and minima in the list below. The following special instructions apply to this army:

- Commanders should be depicted as Timariots.

Ghazi

6

EARLY OTTOMAN TURKISH

Territory Types: Agricultural, Hilly

C-in-C	Inspired Commander/Field Commander/Troop Commander			80/50/35	1	
Sub-commanders	Field Commander			50	0-2	
	Troop Commander			35	0-3	

Troop name	Troop Type				Capabilities		Points per base	Bases per BG	Total bases
	Type	Armour	Quality	Training	Shooting	Close Combat			
Core Troops									
Timariots	Cavalry	Armoured	Superior	Undrilled	Bow	Swordsmen	18	4-6	0-12
		Armoured	Average				14		
		Protected	Superior				14		
		Protected	Average				11		
Ghazis	Light Horse	Unprotected	Superior	Undrilled	Bow	Swordsmen	12	4-6	18-60
			Average				10		
	Cavalry	Unprotected	Superior	Undrilled	Bow	Swordsmen	12		
		Unprotected	Average				10		
		Protected	Superior				14		
		Protected	Average				11		
Azab archers	Medium Foot	Unprotected	Average	Undrilled	Bow	—	5	6-8	6-16
			Poor				3		
	Light Foot	Unprotected	Average	Undrilled	Bow	—	5	6-8	
			Poor				3		
Optional Troops									
Azab slingers	Light Foot	Unprotected	Average	Undrilled	Sling	—	4	4	
			Poor				2		
Azab crossbowmen	Medium Foot	Unprotected	Average	Undrilled	Crossbow	—	5	4	0-4
			Poor				3		
Azab javelinmen	Light Foot	Unprotected	Average	Undrilled	Javelins	Light Spear	4	4	
			Poor				2		
Spearmen	Heavy or Medium Foot	Protected	Average	Undrilled	—	Defensive Spearmen	6	4-6	0-6
			Poor				4		
Poorly equipped levies	Mob	Unprotected	Poor	Undrilled	—	—	2	6-8	0-8
Fortified camp							24		0-1

EARLY OTTOMAN TURKISH ALLIES

Allied commander	Field Commander/Troop Commander						40/25	1	
Troop name	Troop Type				Capabilities		Points per base	Bases per BG	Total bases
	Type	Armour	Quality	Training	Shooting	Close Combat			
Timariots	Cavalry	Armoured	Superior	Undrilled	Bow	Swordsmen	18	4	0-4
		Armoured	Average				14		
		Protected	Superior				14		
		Protected	Average				11		
Ghazis	Light Horse	Unprotected	Superior	Undrilled	Bow	Swordsmen	12		6-16
			Average				10		
	Cavalry	Unprotected	Superior	Undrilled	Bow	Swordsmen	12	4-6	
		Unprotected	Average				10		
		Protected	Superior				14		
		Protected	Average				11		
Azab archers	Medium Foot	Unprotected	Average	Undrilled	Bow	—	5	4-6	0-6
			Poor				3		
	Light Foot	Unprotected	Average	Undrilled	Bow	—	5	4-6	
			Poor				3		

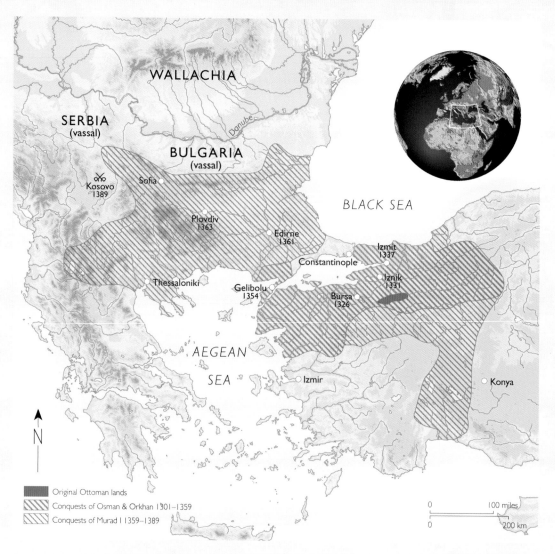

The early Ottoman conquests. Taken from Essential Histories 62: The Ottoman Empire 1326–1699.

LATER OTTOMAN TURKISH

Following the accession of Murad I in 1359, the expansion of the Ottoman Empire gathered momentum. Murad I was recognised as Sultan by the "shadow" caliph in Cairo in 1383. Bulgaria became a vassal state in 1372, Serbia in 1389, Bosnia and Wallachia in 1391. Bulgaria was annexed in 1395. In the east the Anatolian

emirates were conquered, so that by the end of the century the empire stretched from the Euphrates to the Danube. The Byzantine Empire persisted only as tiny enclaves around Constantinople, Salonika and in the Morea (Peloponnese).

In 1402, however, at the Battle of Ankara, the Ottoman army was decisively defeated by Timur

Ottoman troops ford a river, by Angus McBride. Taken from Men-at-Arms 140:
Armies of the Ottoman Turks 1300–1774.

(Tamerlane). Ottoman power in Anatolia collapsed and the seven independent emirates were re-established by Timur. Bosnia and Serbia regained their independence.

A quarter of a century later the Ottoman advance began again. Five of the resurrected Anatolian emirates were annexed between 1426 and 1428. Albania and Byzantine Salonika were conquered in 1430. Constantinople (modern Istanbul), last bastion of the Roman Empire, was captured in 1453. Serbia was finally annexed in 1459, Byzantine Morea in 1460, Bosnia in 1463. Wallachia became a vassal state in 1476. Albania was in revolt from 1443 but finally succumbed in 1479. In the east, the Emirate of Kastamonu and Byzantine Trebizond fell in 1461, the Emirate of Karaman in 1468. The White Sheep Turks were crushingly defeated in 1473 and driven out of Anatolia. The pre-Ankara frontier in the east had been re-established. In 1475 the Genoese colonies in the Crimea were conquered, and the Khanate of the Crimea became a vassal. Expansion continued over the next century.

This list covers the armies of the Ottoman Empire from the accession of Murad I in 1362 AD, until 1500.

QAPU KHALQI

The Qapu Khalqi were the elite guard cavalry of the Ottoman army, forming up around the Sultan.

Qapu Khalqi

JANISSARIES

The corps of Janissaries (from yeniçeri, meaning new soldier) was founded c.1362 by Murad I, and was initially recruited from Christian prisoners of war converted to Islam. By the end of the 14th century a second method of recruitment had been instituted, the devşirme - a levy of boys aged 12 to 16 from the conquered Christian territories. Separated from their families, these boys largely converted to Islam. Their own children would be Muslims and hence not eligible to become Janissaries, thus preventing the development of hereditary ties within the corps. Thus, in theory at least, the Janissary corps gave the Ottoman Sultans an unswervingly loyal standing army. The majority of Janissaries were bow armed until the end of our period.

TIMARIOTS

The bulk of the heavy cavalry (sipahis) in the Ottoman army were supplied on a feudal basis by timariots. Each timariot held a non-hereditary land grant (timar), for which, depending on the value of his timar, he was expected to supply a specified number of fully equipped cavalrymen.

LIGHT CAVALRY

Akinjis ("raiders") were fast-moving lightly equipped bow armed cavalry, descendants of former Turcoman ghazis settled in border regions. They served under their own hereditary leaders. They were used as scouts, raiders and as the vanguard of

Akinji

Byzantine officer surrendering to a Nefer Janissary soldier, by Christa Hook. Taken from Elite 58:
The Janissaries.

the army in battle. Balkan light cavalry lancers were recruited from converts or supplied by Christian tributary states. Djanbazan ("daredevils") were elite akinjis and Delis ("mad-heads") were elite Balkan cavalry. Turcomans, Tatars, Bedouin and Kurds were also used.

AZABS

Azabs ("bachelors") were lightly equipped Turkish infantry, recruited in large numbers for the duration of each campaign.

OTTOMAN TACTICS

By the 15th century the Ottomans had developed a standard battle deployment. In front were the skirmish lines of akinjis and azabs. The main battle line consisted of a central field fortification defended by Janissaries and, later in the century, guns. The Rumelian (European) timariots were deployed outside the fortification on one flank and the Anatolian timariots on the other. The Qapu Khalqi, with the Sultan, were held back in reserve behind the centre. Attacking the strong central defensive position head on was a fundamental mistake that was nevertheless made by many of the Ottomans' opponents, such as the Hungarian army at the second battle of Kosovo in 1448.

LATER OTTOMAN TURKISH STARTER ARMY

Commander-in-Chief	1	Field Commander
Sub-commanders	2	2 x Troop Commander
Qapu Khalqi cavalry	1 BG	4 bases of Qapu Khalqi cavalry: Superior, Armoured, Drilled Cavalry – Bow, Swordsmen
Timariots	2 BGs	Each comprising 4 bases of timariots: Superior, Armoured, Undrilled Cavalry – Bow, Swordsmen
Akinjis	2 BGs	Each comprising 4 bases of akinjis: Average, Unprotected, Undrilled Light Horse – Bow
Janissaries	2 BGs	Each comprising 6 bases of janissaries: Superior, Protected, Drilled, Medium Foot – Bow, Swordsmen
Azabs	2 BGs	Each comprising 8 bases of azabs: Poor, Unprotected, Undrilled Light Foot – Bow
Field fortifications	9	
Camp	1	Unfortified camp
Total	9 BGs	Camp, 20 mounted bases, 20 foot bases, 3 commanders

BUILDING A CUSTOMISED LIST USING OUR ARMY POINTS

Choose an army based on the maxima and minima in the list below. The following special instructions apply to this army:

- Commanders should be depicted as Qapu Khalqi cavalry or Timariots.

- The minima marked * apply only if the Sultan is present.
- Serbian allies cannot include foot.

Ottoman Commander

LATER OTTOMAN TURKISH

Territory Types: Agricultural, Hilly, Developed

C-in-C		Inspired Commander/Field Commander/Troop Commander					80/50/35		1
Sub-commanders		Field Commander					50		0–2
		Troop Commander					35		0–3

Troop name	Troop Type				Capabilities		Points per base	Bases per BG	Total bases
	Type	Armour	Quality	Training	Shooting	Close Combat			
Core Troops									
Qapu Khalqi cavalry	Cavalry	Armoured	Elite	Drilled	Bow	Swordsmen	22	2–6	*2–6
			Superior				19		
Timariots	Cavalry	Armoured	Superior	Undrilled	Bow	Swordsmen	18	4–6	8–24
		Armoured	Average				14		
		Protected	Superior				14		
		Protected	Average				11		
Akinjis	Light Horse	Unprotected	Average	Undrilled	Bow	–	8	4–6	6–30
Janissaries	Medium Foot	Protected	Superior	Drilled	Bow	Swordsmen	10	6–8	*6–16
		Unprotected					8		
Azab archers	Medium Foot	Unprotected	Average	Undrilled	Bow	–	5	6–8	6–16
			Poor				3		
	Light Foot	Unprotected	Average	Undrilled	Bow	–	5	6–8	
			Poor				3		
Optional Troops									
Djanbazan	Light Horse	Unprotected	Superior	Undrilled	Bow	Swordsmen	12	4–6	0–8
Delis	Light Horse	Unprotected	Superior	Undrilled	–	Lancers, Swordsmen	10	4–6	
Other Balkan cavalry	Light Horse	Unprotected	Average	Undrilled	–	Lancers, Swordsmen	8	4–6	
Turcomans or Crimean Tatars	Light Horse	Unprotected	Average	Undrilled	Bow	Swordsmen	10	4–6	0–12
	Cavalry	Unprotected	Average	Undrilled	Bow	Swordsmen	10		
		Protected					11		
Bedouin	Light Horse	Unprotected	Average	Undrilled	–	Lancers, Swordsmen	8	4–6	0–12
	Cavalry	Unprotected	Average	Undrilled	–	Lancers, Swordsmen	8		
		Protected					9		
Kurds	Cavalry	Protected	Average	Undrilled	–	Lancers, Swordsmen	9	4–6	
Janissary slingers	Light Foot	Unprotected	Superior	Drilled	Sling	–	5	4	
Janissary crossbowmen	Medium Foot	Unprotected	Superior	Drilled	Crossbow	–	6	4	
Janissary handgunners	Only from 1430	Light Foot	Unprotected	Superior	Drilled	Firearm	–	5	4
Azab slingers	Light Foot	Unprotected	Average	Undrilled	Sling	–	4	4	0–8
			Poor				2		
Azab crossbowmen	Medium Foot	Unprotected	Average	Undrilled	Crossbow	–	5	4	
			Poor				3		
Azab javelinmen	Light Foot	Unprotected	Average	Undrilled	Javelins	Light Spear	4	4	
			Poor				2		
Azab handgunners	Only from 1430	Light Foot	Unprotected	Average	Undrilled	Firearm	–	4	4
				Poor				2	
Spearmen	Heavy or Medium Foot	Protected	Average	Undrilled	–	Defensive Spearmen	6	4–6	0–6
			Poor				4		
Poorly equipped levies	Mob	Unprotected	Poor	Undrilled	–	–	2	8–12	0–12
Balkan voynuks	Heavy Foot	Armoured	Average	Undrilled	–	Heavy Weapon	9	4	0–4

Iaylars	Medium Foot	Protected	Superior	Undrilled	–	Impact foot, Swordsmen	9	4	0–4
Heavy guns	Heavy artillery	–	Average	Undrilled	Heavy Artillery	–	20	2	0–4
Light guns	Light artillery	–	Average	Undrilled	Light Artillery	–	15	2	
Field defenses	FF						3		0–20
Fortified camp							24		0–1
Allies									
Albanian allies (Only before 1479)									
Crimean Tatar allies (Only from 1475) – Tatar									
Serbian allies (Only before 1459) – Later Serbian									
Anatolian Turkoman allies (Only before 1468)									
Wallachian allies									

LATER OTTOMAN TURKISH ALLIES

Allied commander	Field Commander/Troop Commander						40/25	1	
Troop name	**Troop Type**				**Capabilities**		**Points per base**	**Bases per BG**	**Total bases**
	Type	Armour	Quality	Training	Shooting	Close Combat			
Qapu Khalqi cavalry	Cavalry	Armoured	Elite	Drilled	Bow	Swordsmen	22	2	0–2
			Superior				19		
Timariots	Cavalry	Armoured	Superior	Undrilled	Bow	Swordsmen	18	4–6	4–8
		Armoured	Average				14		
		Protected	Superior				14		
		Protected	Average				11		
Akinjis	Light Horse	Unprotected	Average	Undrilled	Bow	–	8	4–6	4–12
Balkan cavalry	Light Horse	Unprotected	Average	Undrilled	–	Lancers, Swordsmen	8	4–6	0–6
Janissaries	Medium Foot	Protected	Superior	Drilled	Bow	Swordsmen	10	4–6	0–6
		Unprotected					8		
Azab archers	Medium Foot	Unprotected	Average	Undrilled	Bow	–	5	4–6	4–6
			Poor				3		
	Light Foot	Unprotected	Average	Undrilled	Bow	–	5	4–6	
			Poor				3		

ANATOLIAN TURCOMAN ALLIES

This list covers allied contingents supplied by the independent Turkish emirates of Anatolia.

- Commanders should be depicted as heavy cavalry.

Turcoman Heavy Cavalry

ANATOLIAN TURCOMAN ALLIES

Allied commander			Field Commander/Troop Commander				40/25		1
Troop name	Troop Type				Capabilities		Points per base	Bases per BG	Total bases
	Type	Armour	Quality	Training	Shooting	Close Combat			
Heavy cavalry	Cavalry	Armoured	Superior	Undrilled	Bow	Swordsmen	18	4–6	0–6
		Protected					14		
Light cavalry	Light Horse	Unprotected	Average	Undrilled	Bow	Swordsmen	10	4–6	6–18
	Cavalry	Unprotected	Average	Undrilled	Bow	Swordsmen	10		
		Protected					11		
Foot archers	Medium Foot	Unprotected	Average	Undrilled	Bow	-	5	4–6	0–6
			Poor				3		
	Light Foot	Unprotected	Average	Undrilled	Bow	-	5	4–6	
			Poor				3		
Spearmen	Medium Foot	Protected	Average	Undrilled	-	Defensive Spearmen	6	4–6	0–6
			Poor				4		

TATAR

The Golden Horde was a Mongol khanate occupying a huge area of modern Russia, Ukraine, Kazakhstan, and the Caucasus following the division of the Mongol Empire in the 1240s. After the death of Ghengis Khan in 1227, command of the Mongol forces in South Russia was divided between Ghengis's grandsons, the brothers Batu in the west (Blue Horde) and Orda in the east (White Horde). Batu had the larger forces, mostly recruited from conquered tribes, including Cumans (Polovtsy), Alans, Bashkirs, Burtas, Circassians, Karburdians, Kirghiz, Khwarazmians, Mordvins, Volga Bulgars and others.

Between 1236 and 1239, Batu's forces subjugated the Volga Bulgars and the Russian principalities. The latter retained vassal status rather than being directly incorporated into the Horde's territories.

In 1241 Mongol forces invaded central Europe. Batu's forces (under the supreme command of the Great Khan's general Subutai) invaded Hungary, while Orda's forces invaded Poland. The Hungarians were severely defeated at Mohi and the Poles at Liegnitz. Fortunately for Europe, the Great Khan, Ögedei, died the same year, and the

Mongol leaders broke off the campaign to take part in the election of a new Great Khan.

After his return in 1242, Batu established his capital at Sarai, on the lower Volga. Following Batu's death in 1255, the Blue and White Hordes were consolidated into a single state by Batu's brother and successor, Berke. This state came to be known as the Golden Horde, and was the longest lasting of the Mongol successor states. "Tatar" came to be the general term used for its multi-ethnic population.

Despite Russian attempts at conversion to Christianity, the Golden Horde remained pagan until Uzbeg Khan (1312–1341) adopted Islam as the state religion. The Horde's vassal states - including the Russian principalities, Georgia, Alania, the Crimean Greeks and Crimean Goths, were allowed autonomy provided that they continued to pay tribute.

The Russian principalities were

Tatar Cavalry

played off against each other and subject to punitive raids if they got out of line. From the early 14th century the Golden Horde supported Muscovy as the leading Russian principality by granting it the responsibility for collecting all tribute due to the Horde from the whole of Russia.

In the mid-14th century civil war weakened the Horde, allowing the vassal states to assert more independence, and Lithuania and Poland to expand eastwards at the Horde's expense. A Tatar attempt to reassert the Horde's authority in Russia was defeated by the Russians at the Vozha River (1378) and Kulikovo (1380). However, under a new Khan, Tokhtamysh, Moscow was sacked in 1382.

In 1389, however, Tokhtamysh made the foolish mistake of attacking Timur (Tamerlane), suffering successive defeats and destruction of his capital. Nevertheless, in 1399, after dethroning Tokhtamysh, the Horde was sufficiently recovered to defeat the Lithuanians (who were attempting to put him back on the throne) at the Vorskla River.

In the 1440s, civil war began again, and the Horde broke up into eight separate Khanates: The Siberian Khanate, the Qasim Khanate, the Khanate of Kazan, the Khanate of Astrakhan, the Kazakh Khanate, the Uzbek Khanate, the Khanate of Crimea and the last remnant of the Golden Horde - the Great Horde. Muscovite Russia finally broke free of Tatar control by 1480, and thereafter gradually annexed most of the Tatar khanates over the following centuries. The Crimean Khanate became an Ottoman vassal in 1475, although under Ottoman protection it expanded to subjugate the residue of the Great Horde by 1502, and was not itself annexed by Russia until 1783.

This list covers Tatar armies from 1242 until 1500.

TROOP NOTES

Naffatun were armed with naphtha bombs – the medieval equivalent of Molotov cocktails.

TATAR STARTER ARMY		
Commander-in-Chief	1	Field Commander
Sub-commanders	2	2 x Troop Commander
Best equipped cavalry	2 BGs	Each comprising 4 bases of best equipped cavalry: Superior, Armoured, Drilled Cavalry – Bow, Swordsmen
Other cavalry	4 BGs	Each comprising 4 bases of other cavalry: Superior, Protected, Drilled Cavalry – Bow, Swordsmen
Other cavalry	2 BGs	Each comprising 4 bases of other cavalry: Average, Unprotected, Drilled Light Horse – Bow, Swordsmen
Camp	1	Unfortified camp
Total	8 BGs	Camp, 32 mounted bases, 3 commanders

BUILDING A CUSTOMISED LIST USING OUR ARMY POINTS

Choose an army based on the maxima and minima in the list below. The following special instructions apply to this army:

- Commanders should be depicted as best equipped cavalry.

Tatar heavy cavalryman, by Wayne Reynolds. Taken from *Warrior 84: Mongol Warrior 1200–1350.*

TATAR

Territory Types: Agricultural, Steppes

C-in-C	Inspired Commander/Field Commander/Troop Commander						80/50/35	1	
Sub-commanders	Field Commander						50	0–2	
	Troop Commander						35	0–3	

Troop name	Troop Type				Capabilities		Points per base	Bases per BG	Total bases
	Type	Armour	Quality	Training	Shooting	Close Combat			
Core Troops									
Best equipped cavalry	Cavalry	Armoured	Superior	Drilled	Bow	Swordsmen	19	4–6	0–18
				Undrilled			18		
Other cavalry	Light Horse	Unprotected	Superior	Drilled or Undrilled	Bow	Swordsmen	12	4–6	16–72
			Average				10		
	Cavalry	Unprotected	Superior	Drilled	Bow	Swordsmen	13	4–6	
		Unprotected	Superior	Undrilled			12		
		Unprotected	Average	Drilled			11		
		Unprotected	Average	Undrilled			10		
		Protected	Superior	Drilled			15		
		Protected	Superior	Undrilled			14		
		Protected	Average	Drilled			12		
		Protected	Average	Undrilled			11		
Optional Troops									
Armenian or Moslem foot archers	Medium Foot	Unprotected	Average	Undrilled	Bow	–	5	6–8	0–12
			Poor				3		
Naffatun	Only from 1340	Light Foot	Unprotected	Average	Undrilled	Firearm	–	4	4	0–4
Fortified camp							24		0–1
Allies									

Only Golden Horde

Georgian allies (Only before 1259) – See Field of Glory Companion 4: *Swords and Scimitars: The Crusades*

Russian subject allies – Later Russian

Only Crimean Khanate

Ottoman Turkish allies – Later Ottoman Turkish

TATAR ALLIES

Allied commander	Field Commander/Troop Commander						40/25	1	
Troop name	Troop Type				Capabilities		Points per base	Bases per BG	Total bases
	Type	Armour	Quality	Training	Shooting	Close Combat			
Best equipped cavalry	Cavalry	Armoured	Superior	Drilled	Bow	Swordsmen	19	4–6	0–6
				Undrilled			18		
Other cavalry	Light Horse	Unprotected	Superior	Drilled or Undrilled	Bow	Swordsmen	12	4–6	6–18
			Average				10		
	Cavalry	Unprotected	Superior	Drilled	Bow	Swordsmen	13	4–6	
		Unprotected	Superior	Undrilled			12		
		Unprotected	Average	Drilled			11		
		Unprotected	Average	Undrilled			10		
		Protected	Superior	Drilled			15		
		Protected	Superior	Undrilled			14		
		Protected	Average	Drilled			12		
		Protected	Average	Undrilled			11		

LATE BYZANTINE

This list covers Byzantine armies from the recovery of Constantinople in 1261 AD. Armies can be either that of the Central Imperial state based at Constantinople (modern Istanbul), the Despotate of Epiros (in Albania and north-west Greece), the Despotate of the Morea (in the Greek Peloponnese), or the "Empire" of Trebizond (based at modern Trabzon on the south-east Black Sea coast). The Despotate of Epiros was conquered by the central state in 1340. Constantinople did not fall to the Turks until 1453, but no field army was available to the central state after the end of the 14th century. The Despotate of the Morea was semi-independent from 1349, and finally fell to the Turks in 1460. Trebizond fell to the Turks in 1461.

TROOP NOTES

Kavallarioi were probably the descendants of Frankish mercenary knights. Sources of horse archers included Cumans, Turks, Alans, Vlachs, Bulgars, Lazoi and Tzanoi, depending on local availability. Sources of irregular foot included Vlachs, Slavs, Albanians, Lazoi and Tzanoi.

LATE BYZANTINE (CENTRAL) STARTER ARMY		
Commander-in-Chief	1	Field Commander
Sub-commanders	2	2 x Troop Commander
Vardariot guards	1 BG	4 bases of Vardariot guards: Superior, Unprotected, Drilled Cavalry – Bow, Swordsmen
Catalan foot guards	1 BG	6 bases of Catalan foot guards: Superior, Protected, Drilled Medium Foot – Impact Foot, Swordsmen
Kavallarioi	1 BG	4 bases of kavallarioi: Superior, Heavily Armoured, Drilled Knights – Lancers, Swordsmen
Byzantine cavalry	2 BGs	Each comprising 4 bases of Byzantine cavalry: Average, Armoured, Drilled Cavalry – Lancers, Swordsmen
Irregular horse archers	2 BGs	Each comprising 4 bases of irregular horse archers: Average, Unprotected, Drilled Light Horse – Bow, Swordsmen
Regular foot archers	2 BGs	Each comprising 8 bases of regular foot archers: Average, Unprotected, Drilled Light Foot – Bow
Camp	1	Unfortified camp
Total	9 BGs	Camp, 24 mounted bases, 22 foot bases, 3 commanders

BUILDING A CUSTOMISED LIST USING OUR ARMY POINTS

Choose an army based on the maxima and minima in the list below. The following special instructions apply to this army:

- Commanders should be depicted as Byzantine cavalry.

- The minimum marked * does not apply to Central armies.

Irregular Horse archer

Byzantine Soldiers, 14th century, by Angus McBride. Taken from Men-at-Arms 287: Byzantine Armies, AD 1118–1461.

LATE BYZANTINE

Territory Types: Agricultural, Developed, Hilly

C-in-C	Inspired Commander/Field Commander/Troop Commander						80/50/35		1
Sub-commanders	Field Commander						50		0-2
	Troop Commander						35		0-3

Troop name		Troop Type				Capabilities		Points per base	Bases per BG	Total bases
		Type	Armour	Quality	Training	Shooting	Close Combat			
Core Troops										
Kavallarioi	Only Central	Knights	Heavily armoured	Superior	Drilled	–	Lancers, Swordsmen	26	4	0-4
				Average				21		
Byzantine cavalry	Any except Trebizond	Cavalry	Armoured	Average	Drilled	–	Lancers, Swordsmen	13	4-6	6-16
			Armoured	Poor				10		
			Protected	Average				10		
			Protected	Poor				8		
	Only Trebizond before 1400	Cavalry	Armoured	Superior	Drilled	–	Lancers, Swordsmen	17	4-6	
			Armoured	Average				13		
			Protected	Superior				13		
			Protected	Average				10		
	Only Trebizond from 1360	Cavalry	Armoured	Superior	Drilled	Bow	Swordsmen	19	4-6	
			Armoured	Average				15		
			Protected	Superior				15		
			Protected	Average				12		
Irregular horse archers	Any except Morea	Light Horse	Unprotected	Average	Undrilled	Bow	Swordsmen	10	4-6	6-30
		Cavalry	Unprotected	Average	Undrilled	Bow	Swordsmen	10		
			Protected					11		
Regular archers		Medium Foot	Unprotected	Average	Drilled	Bow	–	6	6-8	6-24
				Poor				4		
		Light Foot	Unprotected	Average	Drilled	Bow	–	5	6-8	
				Poor				3		
		Medium Foot	Protected	Average	Drilled	Bow	–	7	6-8	0-12 · 12-72
				Poor				5		
Irregular archers		Medium Foot	Unprotected	Average	Undrilled	Bow	–	5	6-8	*6-48
				Poor				3		
		Light Foot	Unprotected	Average	Undrilled	Bow	–	5	6-8	
				Poor				3		
Optional Troops										
Vardariotai guards	Only Central	Light Horse	Unprotected	Superior	Drilled	Bow	Swordsmen	12	4-6	0-6
		Cavalry	Unprotected	Superior	Drilled	Bow	Swordsmen	13		
			Protected					15		
Tzakones foot guards	Only Central	Medium Foot	Protected	Superior	Drilled	–	Light Spear, Swordsmen	9	4-6	
Catalan foot guards	Only Central	Medium Foot	Protected	Superior	Drilled	–	Offensive Spearmen	10	4-6	0-6
		Medium Foot	Protected	Superior	Drilled	–	Impact Foot, Swordsmen	10		
Byzantine spearmen		Heavy Foot	Protected	Average	Drilled	–	Defensive Spearmen	7	6-8	0-8
				Poor				5		
Hillmen	Any except Central	Medium Foot	Protected	Average	Undrilled	–	Light Spear	5	6-8	0-24
				Poor				3		
		Light Foot	Unprotected	Average	Undrilled	Javelins	Light Spear	4	6-8	
				Poor				2		

Albanian cavalry	Only Epiros	Light Horse	Unprotected	Average	Undrilled	Javelins	Light Spear, Swordsmen	9	4–6	0–8
		Cavalry	Unprotected	Average	Undrilled	–	Light Spear, Swordsmen	8		
			Protected					9		
	Only Morea	Light Horse	Unprotected	Average	Undrilled	Javelins	Light Spear, Swordsmen	9	4–6	0–32
		Cavalry	Unprotected	Average	Undrilled	–	Light Spear, Swordsmen	8		
			Protected					9		
Frankish vassals	Only Morea	Knights	Heavily Armoured	Superior	Undrilled	–	Lancers, Swordsmen	23	4	0–4
Frankish mercenaries	Only Epiros	Knights	Heavily Armoured	Superior	Undrilled	–	Lancers, Swordsmen	23	4	0–4
		Knights	Heavily Armoured	Average	Drilled	–	Lancers, Swordsmen	21		
Fortified camp								24		0–1

Allies

Only Central

Alan allies (Only from 1301 to 1305) – Later Alan – See Field of Glory Companion 4: *Swords and Scimitars: The Crusades*

Bulgarian allies (Only from 1327 to 1352) – Later Bulgarian

Mongol Allies (Only from 1282 to 1283) – Tatar

Ottoman Turkish allies (Only from 1348) – Early Ottoman Turkish

Serbian allies (Only from 1327 to 1352) – Later Serbian

Turkish allies (Only before 1348) – Anatolian Turcoman

Only Epiros

Achaian Frankish allies (Only in 1292) – Latin Greece – See Field of Glory Companion 4: *Swords and Scimitars: The Crusades*

Angevin allies (Only from 1276 to 1291) – Sicilian (See page 71)

Byzantine allies (Only from 1309 to 1310) – Late Byzantine (Central)

Only Trebizond

Georgian allies – See Field of Glory Companion 4: *Swords and Scimitars: The Crusades*

Turkish allies (Only from 1360) – Anatolian Turcoman

Only Morea

Ottoman Turkish allies (Only from 1382) – Later Ottoman Turkish

LATE BYZANTINE ALLIES

Allied commander		Field Commander/Troop Commander					40/25		1	
Troop name		Troop Type				Capabilities		Points per base	Bases per BG	Total bases
	Type	Armour	Quality	Training	Shooting	Close Combat				
Byzantine lancers	Cavalry	Armoured	Average	Drilled	–	Lancers, Swordsmen	13	4–6	4–6	
		Armoured	Poor				10			
		Protected	Average				10			
		Protected	Poor				8			
Irregular horse archers	Light Horse	Unprotected	Average	Undrilled	Bow	Swordsmen	10	4–6	4–8	
	Cavalry	Unprotected	Average	Undrilled	Bow	Swordsmen	10			
		Protected			Bow	Swordsmen	11			
Regular archers	Medium Foot	Unprotected	Average	Drilled	Bow	–	6	6–8	0–8	0–8
			Poor				4			
	Light Foot	Unprotected	Average	Drilled	Bow	–	5	6–8		
			Poor				3			
	Medium Foot	Protected	Average	Drilled	Bow	–	7	4	0–4	
			Poor				5			
Irregular archers	Medium Foot	Unprotected	Average	Undrilled	Bow	–	5	6–8	0–8	
			Poor				3			
	Light Foot	Unprotected	Average	Undrilled	Bow	–	5	6–8		
			Poor				3			

LATER RUSSIAN

On the eve of the Mongol invasion, Russia was divided into a number of rival principalities, including the Principalities of Kiev, Vladimir-Suzdal, Chernigov, Halych-Volhynia, Polotsk and Smolensk, and the Republic of Novgorod. Between 1237 and 1239 the Mongols sacked most of the major Russian cities, including Moscow, Vladimir, Kiev and Chernigov. The only major cities to escape destruction were Smolensk, Novgorod and Pskov. The south Russian principalities of Kiev and Chernigov were completely subjugated by the Mongols, the others, with the exception of Novgorod, were reduced to vassal status. Novgorod, though independent, had its own problems with aggression by the Swedes and Teutonic Knights. Halych-Volhynia was eventually absorbed by the Polish-Lithuanian Commonwealth.

Alexander Nevsky, as elected Prince of Novgorod, won notable victories over the Swedes at the Neva in 1240 and the Teutonic Knights at Lake Peipus in 1242. In 1252 he was installed as Grand Prince of Vladimir, which he remained until his death in 1263.

At the time of Mongol invasion, Moscow was an unimportant outpost in the principality of

Novgorod noble and retinue under attack, by Angus McBride. Taken from Men-at-Arms 367: Medieval Russian Armies 1250–1500.

Vladimir-Suzdal. Under the rule of Daniel I, youngest son of Alexander Nevsky, Moscow began to expand. His son Yury, as Prince of Moscow, made an alliance with Uzbeg Khan of the Golden Horde, allowing him to claim the title of Great Prince of Vladimir in 1317, and giving him the responsibility for collecting the tribute due to the Horde from all of Russia. On his death, in 1325, he was succeeded as Prince of Moscow by his brother Ivan I, who continued to collect tribute on behalf of the Tatars. This allowed him to become immensely rich, and to gain regional ascendancy for Moscow. In 1327 the Muscovites assisted the Tatars in suppressing the revolt of Tver, Moscow's main rival. In the same year, the Orthodox

Metropolitan transferred his residence from Kiev to Moscow, further enhancing the principality's prestige. As became the pattern for subsequent Princes of Moscow, in 1328 Ivan was granted the Horde's permission to become Great Prince of Vladimir. His son Simeon succeeded in 1340 and remained loyal to the Horde, who granted him increasing powers as a counter to the threat of Lithuanian expansion. Simeon died of plague in 1353. He was succeeded by his brother Ivan II, who reigned until 1359. On his death, his son Dmitry (Saint Dmitry) succeeded him at the age of nine.

Dmitry was the first Russian ruler to defeat the Tatars, winning victories over the Tatar commander Mamai at the Vozha River (1378)

Muscovite soldiers, by Angus McBride. Taken from Men-at-Arms 367: Medieval Russian Armies 1250–1500.

and Kulikovo (1380). The situation was reversed, however, under the new Khan Tokhtamysh, who sacked Moscow in 1382. Nevertheless Muscovy continued to expand under Dmitri's successors. By 1480 the Great Principality of Moscow had full control of most of ethnic Russia. In 1476 Ivan III ceased all annual tribute to the Tatars. At the time Akhmat Khan, Khan of the Great Horde, was busy with a war against the Crimean Khanate, and did not respond. Four years later, in 1480, Akhmat Khan invaded. He was met at the River Ugra by the army of Muscovy. After a four day stand off in which the Muscovites repelled all attempts by the Tatars to cross the river, the Khan retreated. Following his death in battle against the Nogay Horde in 1481, the Great Horde collapsed and Tatar domination of Russia was finally ended.

In 1500 the Polish-Lithuanians were decisively defeated by the Muscovites at Vedrosha, following which large swathes of territory were ceded to Muscovy.

This list covers Russian armies from c.1265, by which time we assume that horse archer tactics had been universally adopted, until 1500.

TROOP NOTES

Although some of the better equipped cavalry carried lances, they were primarily horse archers so do not have a "Lancers" POA.

LATER RUSSIAN STARTER ARMY		
Commander-in-Chief	1	Field Commander
Sub-commanders	2	2 x Troop Commander
Princes, greater boyars and their retinues	2 BGs	Each comprising 4 bases of greater boyars etc.: Superior, Armoured, Undrilled Cavalry – Bow, Swordsmen
Lesser boyars and their retinues	3 BGs	Each comprising 4 bases of lesser boyars etc.: Average, Armoured, Undrilled Cavalry – Bow, Swordsmen
Tatars or Cossacks	1 BG	4 bases of Tatars or Cossacks: Average, Unprotected, Undrilled Light Horse – Bow, Swordsmen
Spearmen	2 BGs	Each comprising 6 bases of spearmen: Average, Protected, Undrilled Heavy Foot – Defensive Spearmen
Cossack foot archers	1 BG	8 bases of Cossack foot archers: Average, Unprotected, Undrilled Light Foot – Bow
Handgunners	1 BG	4 bases of handgunners: Average, Unprotected, Undrilled Light Foot – Firearm
Camp	1	Unfortified camp
Total	10 BGs	Camp, 24 mounted bases, 24 foot bases, 3 commanders

BUILDING A CUSTOMISED LIST USING OUR ARMY POINTS

Choose an army based on the maxima and minima in the list below. The following special instructions apply to this army:

- Commanders should be depicted as princes, greater boyars and their retinues.

Handgunner

LATER RUSSIAN

Territory Types: Agricultural, Steppes

Troop name		Troop Type				Capabilities		Points per base	Bases per BG	Total bases
C-in-C		Inspired Commander/Field Commander/Troop Commander						80/50/35	1	
Sub-commanders		Field Commander						50	0–2	
		Troop Commander						35	0–3	
		Type	Armour	Quality	Training	Shooting	Close Combat			
Core Troops										
Princes, greater boyars and their retines		Cavalry	Armoured	Superior	Undrilled	Bow	Swordsmen	18	4–6	4–12
Lesser boyars and their retines		Cavalry	Armoured	Superior	Undrilled	Bow	Swordsmen	18	4–6	12–48
				Average				14		
Optional Troops										
Spearmen		Heavy Foot	Protected	Average	Undrilled	–	Defensive Spearmen	6	6–8	0–12
				Poor				4		
Archers		Medium Foot	Unprotected	Average	Undrilled	Bow	–	5	6–8	0–12
				Poor				3		
Tatars or Cossacks	Only from 1380	Light Horse	Unprotected	Average	Undrilled	Bow	Swordsmen	10	4–6	0–12
		Cavalry	Unprotected	Average	Undrilled	Bow	Swordsmen	10		
			Protected					11		
Cossack foot archers	Only from 1380	Light Foot	Unprotected	Average	Undrilled	Bow	–	5	6–8	0–8
Handgunners	Only from 1470	Light Foot	Unprotected	Average	Undrilled	Firearm	–	4	4–6	0–6
Light guns	Only from 1380	Light artillery	–	Average	Undrilled	Light Artillery	–	15	2	0–2
Gulai gorod		FF						3		0–12
Fortified camp								24		0–1
Allies										
Lithuanian allies (Only before 1380) – Later Lithuanian										
Golden Horde allies (Only before 1380) – Tatar										

LATER RUSSIAN ALLIES

Troop name	Troop Type				Capabilities		Points per base	Bases per BG	Total bases
Allied commander	Field Commander/Troop Commander						40/25	1	
	Type	Armour	Quality	Training	Shooting	Close Combat			
Princes, greater boyars and their retines	Cavalry	Armoured	Superior	Undrilled	Bow	Swordsmen	18	4–6	0–6
Lesser boyars and their retines	Cavalry	Armoured	Superior	Undrilled	Bow	Swordsmen	18	4–6	4–12
			Average				14		

LATER SERBIAN

Serbia repudiated Byzantine hegemony on the death of the Emperor Manuel I Komnenos in 1180 AD. Pope Honorius III granted Stefan II a crown in 1217.

Stefan Uroš II Milutin (ruled 1282–1321), expanded Serbian territories, adding parts of Byzantine Macedonia and Albania. He backed up his conquests with dynastic marriages to Byzantine, Bulgarian and Hungarian princesses, marrying five times altogether.

Serbia reached its peak under Stefan Uroš IV Dušan Silni (ruled 1331–1355) who expanded Serbian territories by conquering most of the Balkan part of the Byzantine Empire as far as central Greece. He remained on good terms with the

Serbian Commander

Bulgarians and successfully repelled Hungarian attacks. In 1346 he was crowned "Tsar and autocrat of the Serbs and Greeks" having already raised the Serbian Orthodox Church from an autocephalous archbishopric to a patriarchate.

Following defeat by the Ottoman Turks at the battle of Maritsa in 1371, Serbia lost territory and became tributary to the expanding Ottoman state. A further defeat at Kosovo in 1389 resulted in the shrunken remains of the Serbian principalities becoming Ottoman vassals. By 1459 most of Serbia had been annexed by the Turks, only parts of Bosnia and Zeta remaining free. These had all fallen by 1496.

This list covers Serbian armies from 1300 to 1459.

TROOP NOTES

Serbian heavy and light cavalry were charging lancers. Their better equipped heavy cavalry wore full knightly panoply, although armour styles lagged somewhat behind those in Western Europe.

LATER SERBIAN STARTER ARMY		
Commander-in-Chief	1	Field Commander
Sub-commanders	2	2 x Troop Commander
Nobles	1 BG	4 bases of nobles: Superior, Heavily Armoured, Undrilled Knights – Lancers, Swordsmen
Nobles	2 BGs	Each comprising 4 bases of nobles: Superior, Armoured, Undrilled Knights – Lancers, Swordsmen
Light horse	2 BGs	Each comprising 4 bases of light horse: Average, Unprotected, Undrilled Light Horse – Lancers, Swordsmen
Voynuks	1 BG	8 bases of voynuks: Average, Protected, Undrilled Heavy Foot – Heavy Weapon
Archers	3 BGs	Each comprising 6 bases of archers: Average, Unprotected, Undrilled Light Foot – Bow
Handgunners	1 BG	4 bases of handgunners: Average, Unprotected, Drilled Light Foot – Firearm
Camp	1	Unfortified camp
Total	10 BGs	Camp, 20 mounted bases, 30 foot bases, 3 commanders

BUILDING A CUSTOMISED LIST USING OUR ARMY POINTS

Choose an army based on the maxima and minima in the list below. The following special instructions apply to this army:

- Commanders should be depicted as nobles.
- A Bosnian allied general can command only

Bosnian troops, which can include border foot.
- Only one allied contingent can be used.

Serbian Light Horse

LATER SERBIAN

Territory Types: Agricultural, Hilly, Mountains

C-in-C		Inspired Commander/Field Commander/Troop Commander						80/50/35		1
Sub-commanders		Field Commander						50		0–2
		Troop Commander						35		0–3
Bosnian allied commander		Field Commander/Troop Commander						40/25		0–1

Troop name		Troop Type				Capabilities		Points per base	Bases per BG	Total bases
		Type	Armour	Quality	Training	Shooting	Close Combat			
Core Troops										
Serbian or Bosnian nobles	Before 1345	Cavalry	Armoured	Superior	Undrilled	–	Lancers, Swordsmen	16	4–6	12–34
	From 1345	Knights	Heavily Armoured	Superior	Undrilled	–	Lancers, Swordsmen	23	4–6	8–28
			Armoured					20		
Serbian light horse	Only from 1345	Light Horse	Unprotected	Average	Undrilled	–	Lancers, Swordsmen	8	4–6	4–18
Serbian, Bosnian, Croat, Moravian or Greek archers		Medium Foot	Unprotected	Average	Undrilled	Bow	–	5	6–8	8–32
				Poor				3		
		Medium Foot	Protected	Average	Undrilled	Bow	–	6	6–8	
				Poor				4		
		Light Foot	Unprotected	Average	Undrilled	Bow	–	5	6–8	
				Poor				3		
Optional Troops										
Cuman, Hungarian, Tatar or Turcoman mercenaries		Light Horse	Unprotected	Average	Undrilled	Bow	Swordsmen	10	4–6	0–12
		Cavalry	Unprotected	Average	Undrilled	Bow	Swordsmen	10		
			Protected					11		
Wallachian mercenaries		Light Horse	Unprotected	Average	Undrilled	Bow	Light Spear, Swordsmen	11	4–6	0–6
		Cavalry	Unprotected	Average	Undrilled	Bow*	Light Spear, Swordsmen	10		
			Protected					11		
Western mercenary men-at-arms		Knights	Heavily Armoured	Average	Drilled	–	Lancers, Swordsmen	21	4	0–4
Voynuks with spears		Heavy Foot	Armoured	Average	Undrilled	–	Defensive Spearmen	8	6–8	0–8
			Protected					6		
Voynuks with polearms		Heavy Foot	Armoured	Average	Undrilled	–	Heavy Weapon	9	6–8	
			Protected					7		
Border foot with mixed weapons		Medium Foot	Protected	Average	Undrilled	–	Light Spear	5	6–8	0–12
Levies or baggage guards		Mob	Unprotected	Poor	Undrilled	–	–	2	6–8	0–12

Mercenary crossbowmen	Only from 1380	Medium Foot	Protected	Average	Drilled	Crossbow	–	7	4	0–4
Mercenary handgunners		Light Foot	Unprotected	Average	Drilled	Firearm	–	4	4	
			Protected					5		
Light Guns		Light artillery	–	Average	Undrilled	Light Artillery	–	15	2	0–2
Heavy Guns		Heavy artillery	–	Average	Undrilled	Heavy Artillery	–	20	2	

Allies
Only before 1380
Byzantine allies – Late Byzantine
Only from 1380
Albanian allies
Hungarian allies – Middle Hungarian
Ottoman Turkish allies – Later Ottoman Turkish

LATER SERBIAN ALLIES

Allied commander			Field Commander/Troop Commander				40/25		1	
Troop name		Troop Type				Capabilities		Points per base	Bases per BG	Total bases
		Type	Armour	Quality	Training	Shooting	Close Combat			
Serbian or Bosnian nobles	Before 1345	Cavalry	Armoured	Superior	Undrilled	–	Lancers, Swordsmen	16	4–6	4–8
	From 1345	Knights	Heavily Armoured	Superior	Undrilled	–	Lancers, Swordsmen	23	4–6	4–6
			Armoured					20		
Serbian light horse	Only from 1345	Light Horse	Unprotected	Average	Undrilled	–	Lancers, Swordsmen	8	4–6	0–8
Serbian, Bosnian, Croat, Moravian or Greek archers		Medium Foot	Unprotected	Average	Undrilled	Bow	–	5	6–8	0–8
				Poor				3		
		Medium Foot	Protected	Average	Undrilled	Bow	–	6	6–8	
				Poor				4		
		Light Foot	Unprotected	Average	Undrilled	Bow	–	5	6–8	
				Poor				3		

LATER BULGARIAN

This list covers the armies of the "Second Bulgarian Empire" from 1300 AD until its annexation by the Ottoman Turks in 1395. It was an Ottoman vassal from 1372. Although called Bulgarian, the kingdom arose (in 1186) from an alliance of Bulgars, Vlachs & Cumans, and this continued to be reflected in the composition of its armies, which also included Greek troops from the ex-Byzantine cities of Thrace and Macedonia.

LATER BULGARIAN STARTER ARMY

Commander-in-Chief	1	Field Commander
Sub-commanders	2	2 x Troop Commander
Nobles	3 BGs	Each comprising 4 bases of nobles: Superior, Armoured, Undrilled Cavalry – Lancers, Swordsmen
Horse archers	4 BGs	Each comprising 4 bases of horse archers: Average, Unprotected, Undrilled Light Horse – Bow, Swordsmen
Spearmen	1 BG	8 bases of spearmen: Average, Protected, Undrilled Heavy Foot – Defensive Spearmen
Archers	2 BGs	Each comprising 8 bases of archers: Average, Unprotected, Undrilled Light Foot – Bow
Camp	1	Unfortified camp
Total	10 BGs	Camp, 28 mounted bases, 24 foot bases, 3 commanders

BUILDING A CUSTOMISED LIST USING OUR ARMY POINTS

Choose an army based on the maxima and minima in the list below. The following special instructions apply to this army:

- Commanders should be depicted as nobles.
- The minima marked * apply only if any foot are used.

Cuman horse archer

LATER BULGARIAN

Territory Types: Agricultural, Hilly

Troop name							Points per base	Bases per BG	Total bases
C-in-C		Inspired Commander/Field Commander/Troop Commander					80/50/35		1
Sub-commanders		Field Commander					50		0–2
		Troop Commander					35		0–3
	Troop Type				Capabilities		Points per base	Bases per BG	Total bases
	Type	Armour	Quality	Training	Shooting	Close Combat			
Core Troops									
Nobles	Cavalry	Armoured	Superior	Undrilled	–	Lancers, Swordsmen	16	4–6	6–24
Bulgarian, Cuman, Vlach or Hungarian horse archers	Light Horse	Unprotected	Average	Undrilled	Bow	Swordsmen	10	4–6	12–52
	Cavalry	Unprotected	Average	Undrilled	Bow	Swordsmen	10		
		Protected					11		
Bulgarian spearmen	Heavy Foot	Protected	Average	Undrilled	–	Defensive Spearmen	6	6–8	*6–12
			Poor				4		
Bulgarian or Vlach archers	Medium Foot	Unprotected	Average	Undrilled	Bow	–	5	6–8	*6–18
			Poor				3		
	Light Foot	Unprotected	Average	Undrilled	Bow	–	5	6–8	
			Poor				3		
Optional Troops									
Greek cavalry	Cavalry	Protected	Poor	Drilled	–	Lancers, Swordsmen	8	4	0–4
Greek spearmen	Heavy Foot	Protected	Poor	Drilled	–	Defensive Spearmen	5	4–6	0–6
Greek archers	Medium Foot	Unprotected	Poor	Drilled	Bow	–	4	4–6	0–6
Fortified camp							24		0–1

LATER LITHUANIAN

Having successfully resisted attempts at conquest by the Teutonic Knights in the 13th century, the pagan Grand Duchy of Lithuania began to expand. By the end of the reign of Vytenis (1295–1316), Lithuanian territory included Lithuania proper, Samogitia (modern western Lithuania), Red Russia (in western Ukraine) and Polatsk and Minsk (in Belarus). His brother and successor, Gediminas (1316–1341) added the Russian principality of Halych-Volynia and the city of Kiev (in Ukraine). Gediminas's son Algirdas (1345–1377) took the Russian principalities of Smolensk and Bryansk (in western Russia). He defeated the Tatars at the Blue Waters of the Southern Bug in 1362 and extended Lithuanian territory almost to the northern shores of the Black Sea. He besieged Moscow unsuccessfully in 1368 and 1372.

Algirdas's son Jogaila (1377–1434) converted to Christianity in 1386, married the eleven-year-old Queen Jadwiga of Poland, and was crowned Polish king as Władysław II Jagiełło. Thereafter the crowns of Poland and Lithuania were united in personal union, but Lithuania remained a separate state ruled by a Grand Duke (who was often also King of Poland). Władysław was forced to formally recognise his cousin Vytautas as Grand Duke of Lithuania, under his overlordship, in 1401.

Władysław's baptism, while politically inconvenient to the Teutonic Knights, failed to

Lithuanian nobleman (right), by Angus McBride. Taken from **Men-at-Arms 436: The Scandinavian Baltic Crusades 1100–1500.**

end their attacks. They claimed his conversion was a sham and renewed their attacks on the pretext that there were still many pagans in Lithuania. However, at the Battle of Grunwald (Tannenberg) in 1410, the Teutonic Knights were decisively defeated by the combined Polish-Lithuanian army under King Władysław and Grand Duke Vytautas. Poland-Lithuania failed to take full advantage of the magnitude of the Teutonic defeat, and granted generous peace terms, but this nevertheless marked the effective end of a serious Teutonic threat, though the wars were to drag on for many decades.

This list covers Lithuanian armies from 1300 until 1500.

TROOP NOTES

Lithuanian cavalry were equipped with a shortish light "lance" which could be thrust or thrown, and with bow. They were fond of skirmishing and ambushes, and sometimes feigned flight, but they deployed for pitched battle in close order squadrons with the armoured boyars forming the front ranks or centre of each squadron, supported or surrounded by their unarmoured followers. We assume that only the best equipped contingents would have enough armoured men to justify classification as Armoured. We classify the Cavalry as Bow* because they were not specialist horse archers.

LATER LITHUANIAN STARTER ARMY		
Commander-in-Chief	1	Field Commander
Sub-commanders	2	2 x Troop Commander
Lithuanian armoured cavalry	2 BGs	Each comprising 4 bases of Lithuanian armoured cavalry: Superior, Armoured, Undrilled Cavalry – Bow*, Light Spear, Swordsmen
Lithuanian unarmoured cavalry	4 BGs	Each comprising 4 bases of Lithuanian unarmoured cavalry: Average, Unprotected, Undrilled Light Horse – Bow, Light Spear, Swordsmen
Polish knights and strzelcy	1 BG	4 bases of Polish knights and strzelcy: Superior, Heavily Armoured, Undrilled Knights – Lancers, Swordsmen
Archers	2 BGs	Each comprising 6 bases of archers: Average, Unprotected, Undrilled Light Foot – Bow
Camp	1	Unfortified camp
Total	9 BGs	Camp, 28 mounted bases, 12 foot bases, 3 commanders

BUILDING A CUSTOMISED LIST USING OUR ARMY POINTS

Choose an army based on the maxima and minima in the list below. The following special instructions apply to this army:

- Commanders should be depicted as armoured Lithuanian cavalry or (only from 1386) Polish knights.
- Lithuanian light horse or cavalry in a

Lithuanian army can always dismount to defend field fortifications as Medium Foot, Undrilled, Bow, Swordsmen. (Quality and armour class the same as when mounted).

- The minima marked * apply only if any Polish troops are used.
- Only one allied contingent can be used.

Late 15th century heavy gun

LATER LITHUANIAN

Territory Types: Agricultural, Woodlands, Steppes

C-in-C	Inspired Commander/Field Commander/Troop Commander					80/50/35		1		
Sub-commanders	Field Commander					50		0–2		
	Troop Commander					35		0–3		

Troop name	Troop Type				Capabilities		Points per base	Bases per BG	Total bases	
	Type	Armour	Quality	Training	Shooting	Close Combat				
Core Troops										
Lithuanian cavalry	Light Horse	Unprotected	Average	Undrilled	Bow	Light Spear, Swordsmen	11	4–6	16–72	16–80
	Cavalry	Unprotected	Average	Undrilled	Bow*	Light Spear, Swordsmen	10	4–6		
		Protected					11			
	Cavalry	Armoured	Superior	Undrilled	Bow*	Light Spear, Swordsmen	18	4–6	0–18	
Lithuanian spearmen	Medium Foot	Protected	Average	Undrilled	–	Light Spear	5	6–8	0–12	
Lithuanian or (from 1360) Russian archers	Light Foot	Unprotected	Average	Undrilled	Bow	–	5	6–8	0–12	
	Medium foot	Unprotected	Average	Undrilled	Bow	–	5	6–8		
Optional Troops										
Tatar exiles	Light Horse	Unprotected	Average	Undrilled	Bow	Swordsmen	10		0–6	
	Cavalry	Unprotected	Average	Undrilled	Bow	Swordsmen	10	4–6		
		Protected	Average				11			
Russian cavalry	Only from 1360	Cavalry	Armoured	Superior	Undrilled	Bow	Swordsmen	18	4–6	0–12
				Average				14		
Polish knights and strzelcy	Only from 1386	Knights	Heavily Armoured	Superior	Undrilled	–	Lancers, Swordsmen	23	1/2 or all	*4–12
		Cavalry	Armoured	Superior	Undrilled	Crossbow	Swordsmen	17	1/2 or 0 4–6	*4–12
			Protected					13	0–6	
Separately deployed Polish strzelcy	Only from 1386	Cavalry	Armoured	Average	Undrilled	Crossbow	Swordsmen	13	4–6	0–6
			Protected					10		
Teutonic knights	Only from 1397	Knights	Heavily Armoured	Superior	Drilled	–	Lancers, Swordsmen	26	4	0–4
Heavy guns	Only from 1382	Heavy Artillery	–	Average	Undrilled	Heavy Artillery	–	20	2	0–2
Field fortifications	FF							3		0–12
Fortified camp								24		0–1
Allies										
Golden Horde or Crimean Tatar allies – Tatar										
Special Campaigns										
Only Švitrigaila in 1435										
Hussite war wagons and crew	Battle Wagons	–	Average	Undrilled	Crossbow	Heavy Weapon	23	2–4	0–6	
Teutonic Knight allies – Later Teutonic Knights										
No Polish troops are permitted. Teutonic Knight allies are compulsory and are used in place of the Teutonic Knights normally allowed within the list.										

LATER LITHUANIAN ALLIES

Allied commander			Field Commander/Troop Commander					40/25		1	
Troop name	**Troop Type**				**Capabilities**		**Points per base**	**Bases per BG**	**Total bases**		
	Type	Armour	Quality	Training	Shooting	Close Combat					
Lithuanian cavalry	Light Horse	Unprotected	Average	Undrilled	Bow	Light Spear, Swordsmen	11	4–6	6–18	6–18	
	Cavalry	Unprotected	Average	Undrilled	Bow*	Light Spear, Swordsmen	10	4–6			
		Protected					11				
	Cavalry	Armoured	Superior	Undrilled	Bow*	Light Spear, Swordsmen	18	4–6	0–6		
Lithuanian spearmen	Medium Foot	Protected	Average	Undrilled	–	Light Spear	5	4	0–4		
Lithuanian archers	Light Foot	Unprotected	Average	Undrilled	Bow	–	5	4	0–4		
	Medium foot	Unprotected	Average	Undrilled	Bow	–	5	4			

Lithuanian cavalry charge the Teutonic Knights at Tannenberg, by Richard Hook. Taken from Campaign 122: Tannenberg 1410.

LATER POLISH

In the 12th and 13th centuries Poland was fragmented between rival scions of the Piast dynasty. Władysław I the Elbow-High reunited much of the country in the early decades of the 14th century and was crowned King in 1320. His son, Casimir III the Great (1333–1370), continued his father's work, expanding Poland's territories in the east. Dying without legitimate sons, he named Louis I the Angevin King of Hungary as his heir. The latter's daughter Jadwiga, his successor in Poland, married Jogaila, Grand Duke of Lithuania, in 1386, thus uniting the thrones of Poland and Lithuania in personal union. Jogaila converted to Christianity and became Władysław II Jagiełło, founding the Jagiellon dynasty which ruled until 1572. The territories of Poland-Lithuania stretched from the Baltic Sea and Carpathian Mountains to modern Belarus and western and central Ukraine.

The Teutonic Knights were defeated in the Battle of Grunwald (Tannenberg) in 1410, the Gollub War in 1422, the Polish-Teutonic War of

Polish troops besiege a castle, by Gerry Embleton. Taken from Men-at-Arms 445: Medieval Polish Armies.

1431–1435 and the Thirteen Years War of 1454–1466. By the Second Treaty of Toruń (Thorn) of 1466, the Teutonic Order lost much of its territory, including West Prussia, which was ceded to Poland, and had to accept Polish suzerainty over its remaining territories in East Prussia.

In 1440, Jogaila's son King Władysław III (1434–1444) accepted the throne of Hungary, thus bringing Poland into the on-going struggle against the Ottoman Turks. He took part in the Hungaro-Polish victory over the Turks at Nish in 1443, but was killed in the defeat at Varna in 1444. He was succeeded in Poland by his brother Casimir IV (1447–1492) after a 3-year interregnum. In Hungary he was succeeded by his former rival, Ladislaus Posthumus.

Casimir's son Jan I Olbracht (1492–1501) gathered another Crusading army to attack the Turks, but, instead came into conflict with Ştefan the Great of Moldavia, and was defeated at the Battle of the Cosmin Forest (1497).

This list covers Polish armies from 1300 to 1500.

TROOP NOTES

In the earlier part of the period, the knights were usually drawn up in a continuous line, usually 4 deep, with a second line of mounted crossbowmen (strzelcy – the knights' retainers) behind. Later, the battle line was organised into a number of separate banners, with gaps between. Each banner consisted of strzelcy surrounded by men-at-arms. The strzelcy shot from horse-back by volley to soften up the enemy prior to the charge.

After the start, in 1454, of the 13 years war against the Teutonic Order, standing companies were raised to replace the general feudal knightly levy. These had proved a liability by refusing to fight until the king agreed to their political demands, and then losing against a smaller force of Teutonics. In peacetime, a relatively small standing army was maintained, mainly in the eastern provinces, but in wartime their numbers were increased. They were categorised as Lancer banners or Volley banners. Lancer banners contained men-at-arms and mounted crossbowmen in the approximate ratio of 1:2. In Volley banners the ratio was more like 1:4 or 1:5.

Battle groups with a substantial proportion of lancers are treated as Superior. Where the proportion of strzelcy is higher, the battle group is treated as Average. The armour of later men-at-arms became progressively lighter as some strzelcy replaced their crossbows with lances, and gentry increasingly replaced knights.

LATER POLISH STARTER ARMY		
Commander-in-Chief	1	Field Commander
Sub-commanders	2	2 x Troop Commander
Feudal nobles	3 BGs	Each comprising 4 bases of feudal nobles: Superior, Heavily Armoured, Undrilled Knights – Lancers, Swordsmen
Separately deployed strzelcy	3 BGs	Each comprising 4 bases of separately deployed strzelcy: Average, Protected, Undrilled Cavalry – Crossbow, Swordsmen
Lithuanian cavalry	1 BG	4 bases of Lithuanian cavalry: Average, Unprotected, Undrilled Light Horse – Bow, Light Spear, Swordsmen
Cuman cavalry	1 BG	4 bases of Cuman cavalry: Average, Unprotected, Undrilled Light Horse – Bow, Swordsmen
Camp	1	Unfortified camp
Total	8 BGs	Camp, 32 mounted bases, 3 commanders

BUILDING A CUSTOMISED LIST USING OUR ARMY POINTS

Choose an army based on the maxima and minima in the list below. The following special instructions apply to this army:

- Commanders should be depicted as nobles.

- The total number of bases of separately deployed strzelcy cannot exceed the total number of bases of feudal nobles and strzelcy.
- The minimum marked * only applies before 1455, or if any feudal knights or strzelcy are used thereafter.
- The minima marked ** apply from 1455.

LATER POLISH

Territory Types: Agricultural, Woodlands

C-in-C	Inspired Commander/Field Commander/Troop Commander					80/50/35		1	
Sub-commanders	Field Commander					50		0–2	
	Troop Commander					35		0–3	
Troop name	Troop Type				Capabilities		Points per base	Bases per BG	Total bases
	Type	Armour	Quality	Training	Shooting	Close Combat			
Core Troops									
Feudal nobles and strzelcy	Knights	Heavily Armoured	Superior	Undrilled	–	Lancers, Swordsmen	23	1/2 or all	*6–24
	Cavalry	Armoured	Superior	Undrilled	Crossbow	Swordsmen	17	1/2 or 0	0–24
		Protected					13		
Separately deployed strzelcy	Cavalry	Armoured	Average	Undrilled	Crossbow	Swordsmen	13	4–6	0–16
		Protected					10		
Lancer banners	Only from 1455	Knights	Heavily Armoured	Superior	Drilled	–	Lancers, Swordsmen	26	1/2	**4–18
		Cavalry	Armoured	Superior	Drilled	–	Lancers, Swordsmen	17		
		Cavalry	Armoured	Superior	Drilled	Crossbow	Swordsmen	18	1/2	
Volley banners	Only from 1455	Cavalry	Armoured	Average	Drilled	Crossbow	Swordsmen	14	4–6	**4–18
Lithuanian cavalry		Light Horse	Unprotected	Average	Undrilled	Bow	Light Spear, Swordsmen	11	4–6	0–6 before 1386, 0–24 from 1386
		Cavalry	Unprotected	Average	Undrilled	Bow*	Light Spear, Swordsmen	10		
			Protected					11		
Town militia with axes	Heavy Foot	Protected	Average	Drilled	–	Heavy Weapon	8	4–6	0–6
Town militia crossbowmen and pavisiers	Heavy Foot	Protected	Average	Drilled	–	Defensive Spearmen	7	1/2	0–12
	Medium Foot	Protected	Average	Drilled	Crossbow	–	7	1/2	
Optional Troops									
Hungarians, Cumans, Tatars or other mercenary horse archers	Light Horse	Unprotected	Average	Undrilled	Bow	Swordsmen	10	4–6	0–6
	Cavalry	Unprotected	Average	Undrilled	Bow	Swordsmen	10		
		Protected					11		
Serbian hussars	Only from 1386	Light Horse	Unprotected	Average	Undrilled	–	Lancers, Swordsmen	8	4–6	0–6
Handgunners	Only from 1386	Light Foot	Unprotected	Average	Drilled or Undrilled	Firearm	–	4	4	0–4
War wagons	Only from 1386	Battle Wagons	–	Average	Undrilled	Crossbow	Heavy Weapon	23	2–4	0–4
Light guns	Only from 1386	Light Artillery	–	Average	Undrilled	Light Artillery	–	15	2	0–2
Wagon fortress	FF						3		0–20
Fortified camp							24		0–1
Allies									
Hungarian allies (Only before 1445) – Middle or Later Hungarian									
Bohemian allies (Only from 1471 to 1474) – Hussite									

Note: Core Troops total bases 12–48.

LATER POLISH ALLIES									
Allied commander		Field Commander/Troop Commander					40/25		1
Troop name		Troop Type				Capabilities	Points per base	Bases per BG	Total bases
		Type	Armour	Quality	Training	Shooting	Close Combat		

Troop name		Type	Armour	Quality	Training	Shooting	Close Combat	Points per base	Bases per BG	Total bases	
Feudal nobles and strzelcy		Knights	Heavily Armoured	Superior	Undrilled	–	Lancers, Swordsmen	23	1/2 or all	*4–12	4–12
		Cavalry	Armoured	Superior	Undrilled	Crossbow	Swordsmen	17	1/2 or 0	0–6	
			Protected					13			
Separately deployed strzelcy		Cavalry	Armoured	Average	Undrilled	Crossbow	Swordsmen	13	4–6	0–6	
			Protected					10			
Lancer banners	Only from 1455	Knights	Heavily Armoured	Superior	Drilled	–	Lancers, Swordsmen	26	1/2	4–6	0–8
		Cavalry	Armoured	Superior	Drilled	–	Lancers, Swordsmen	17	1/2		
		Cavalry	Armoured	Superior	Drilled	Crossbow	Swordsmen	18	1/2		
Volley banners	Only from 1455	Cavalry	Armoured	Average	Drilled	Crossbow	Swordsmen	14	4–6	0–8	
Lithuanian cavalry	Only from 1386	Light Horse	Unprotected	Average	Undrilled	Bow	Light Spear, Swordsmen	11	4–6	0–8	
		Cavalry	Unprotected	Average	Undrilled	Bow*	Light Spear, Swordsmen	10			
			Protected					11			
Town militia crossbowmen and pavisiers		Heavy Foot	Protected	Average	Drilled	–	Defensive Spearmen	7	1/2	6	0–6
		Medium Foot	Protected	Average	Drilled	Crossbow	–	7	1/2		

LATER TEUTONIC KNIGHTS

The Teutonic Knights or Teutonic Order (The Order of the German House of St. Mary in Jerusalem) was founded as a German hospital order during the siege of Acre in 1190 and transformed into a military order in 1198.

In 1226 Konrad I, Duke of Masovia in west-central Poland, invited the Teutonic Knights to assist in the conquest of the pagan Prussians, granting the Order the use of Chełmno Land (Kulmerland) in modern central Poland as their base.

The Livonian Brothers of the Sword, also recruited from Germany, were founded in 1202 by Albert of Buxhoeveden, Bishop of Riga, with the aim of converting the pagan Curonians, Livonians, Semigallians, and Latgalians along the Gulf of Riga. After a severe defeat by the Lithuanians and Semigallians at the Battle of Schaulen (Saule) in 1236, they were incorporated into the Teutonic Order.

By 1300 the Teutonic Order was well established in Prussia, Latvia, Estonia, and Livonia. In 1309 they annexed Pomerelia (in northern

Teutonic Commanders

Poland, around Gdansk). In 1337 the Holy Roman Emperor Louis IV allegedly granted the Order the right to conquer all Lithuania and Russia.

With the conversion in 1386 of Grand Duke Jogaila of Lithuania and his coronation as King of Poland as Władysław II Jagiełło, the justification for Teutonic attacks on pagan Lithuania was weakened. Initially, however, the Order managed to play off Władysław's cousin Vytautas against him, and by 1407 the Order had reached its greatest territorial extent, including in its domains the lands of Prussia, Pomerelia, Samogitia, Courland, Livonia, Estonia, Gotland, Dagö, Ösel and the Neumark.

However, Vytautas eventually broke with the Order and was reconciled with Władysław. In 1410 the joint Polish-Lithuanian forces under the two cousins inflicted a crushing defeat on the Teutonic Knights at the Battle of Grunwald (Tannenberg). Following this, succeeding conflicts went pretty much Poland's way, the Teutonic Knights losing the Gollub War in 1422, the Polish-Teutonic War of 1431-1435 and the Thirteen Years War of 1454-1466. By the Second Treaty of Toruń (Thorn) of 1466, the Teutonic Order lost much of its territory, including Pomerelia, Chełmno Land and West Prussia, which were ceded to Poland, and had to accept Polish suzerainty over its remaining territories in East Prussia.

In 1525 the Grand Master Albrecht of Prussia adopted Lutheranism and declared himself Duke of Prussia under the overlordship of Poland.

This list covers the armies of the Ordensstaat of the Teutonic Knights from 1300 to 1500.

TROOP NOTES

Subject foot included Estonians, Kurs, Letts, Livs and Prussians. Turcopoles were mercenary or native light cavalry. We have found no evidence for the horse archers included in previous published army lists.

LATER TEUTONIC KNIGHTS STARTER ARMY		
Commander-in-Chief	1	Field Commander
Sub-commanders	2	2 x Troop Commander
Brother knights and sergeants	2 BGs	Each comprising 4 bases of brother knights and sergeants: Superior, Heavily Armoured, Drilled Knights – Lancers, Swordsmen
"Crusader" men-at-arms	1 BG	4 bases of "crusader" men-at-arms: Superior, Heavily Armoured, Undrilled Knights – Lancers, Swordsmen
Turcopoles	1 BG	4 bases of turcopoles: Average, Unprotected, Undrilled Light Horse – Javelins, Light Spear
Mounted crossbowmen	1 BG	4 bases of mounted crossbowmen: Average, Protected, Drilled Cavalry – Crossbow, Swordsmen
Subject foot spearmen	1 BG	8 bases of subject foot spearmen: Average, Protected, Undrilled Medium Foot – Defensive Spearmen
Subject foot archers	1 BG	8 bases of subject foot archers: Average, Unprotected, Undrilled Light Foot – Bow
Handgunners	1 BG	4 bases of Handgunners: Average, Protected, Drilled Light Foot - Firearm
Camp	1	Unfortified camp
Total	8 BGs	Camp, 20 mounted bases, 20 foot bases, 3 commanders

Teutonic Knight raiding party in Lithuania in winter, mid-14th century, by Graham Turner. Taken from *Warrior 124: Teutonic Knight, 1190–1561*.

BUILDING A CUSTOMISED LIST USING OUR ARMY POINTS

Choose an army based on the maxima and minima in the list below. The following special instructions apply to this army:

- Commanders should be depicted as brother knights.
- The minima marked * apply if troops so marked are used.

Teutonic Brother Knights

LATER TEUTONIC KNIGHTS

Territory Types: Agricultural, Woodlands

C-in-C	Inspired Commander/Field Commander/Troop Commander					80/50/35	1	
Sub-commanders	Field Commander					50	0–2	
	Troop Commander					35	0–3	

Troop name	Troop Type				Capabilities		Points per base	Bases per BG	Total bases
	Type	Armour	Quality	Training	Shooting	Close Combat			
Core Troops									
Brother knights and sergeants	Knights	Heavily Armoured	Superior	Drilled	–	Lancers, Swordsmen	26	4–6	4–12
Vassal, "Crusader" or mercenary men-at-arms	Knights	Heavily Armoured	Superior	Undrilled	–	Lancers, Swordsmen	23	4–6	0–12	4–16
	Knights	Heavily Armoured	Average	Drilled	–	Lancers, Swordsmen	21	4–6	0–12
Turcopoles	Light horse	Unprotected	Average	Undrilled	Javelins	Light Spear	7	4–6	4–12
	Cavalry	Protected	Average	Undrilled		Light Spear, Swordsmen	9	4–6	
Serving brother or mercenary spearmen	Heavy Foot	Protected	Average	Drilled	–	Defensive Spearmen	7	4–6	*4–6
Serving brother or mercenary crossbowmen	Medium Foot	Protected	Average	Drilled	Crossbow	–	7	6–8	*6–12
Subject foot spearmen	Medium Foot	Protected	Average	Undrilled	–	Defensive Spearmen	6	6–8	0–8
	Medium Foot	Protected	Poor	Undrilled	–	Defensive Spearmen	4	6–8	0–16
Subject foot archers	Light Foot	Unprotected	Average	Undrilled	Bow	–	5	6–8	0–8
			Poor				3		
Optional Troops									
Mounted crossbowmen	Cavalry	Protected	Average	Drilled	Crossbow	Swordsmen	11	4–6	0–6
German town militia spearmen	Heavy Foot	Protected	Poor	Drilled	–	Defensive Spearmen	5	4–6	0–6
German town militia crossbowmen	Medium Foot	Protected	Poor	Drilled	Crossbow	–	5	4–6	0–6
Vassal or "Crusader" crossbowmen	Medium Foot	Protected	Average	Undrilled	Crossbow	–	6	4–6	
Handgunners	Only from 1380	Light Foot	Unprotected	Average	Drilled	Firearm	–	4	4	0–4
			Protected					5		
Bombards	Only from 1380	Heavy Artillery	–	Average	Undrilled	Heavy Artillery	–	20	2	0–2

LATER TEUTONIC KNIGHTS ALLIES

Allied commander	Field Commander/Troop Commander						40/25		1
Troop name	**Troop Type**				**Capabilities**		**Points per base**	**Bases per BG**	**Total bases**
	Type	Armour	Quality	Training	Shooting	Close Combat			
Brother knights and sergeants	Knights	Heavily Armoured	Superior	Drilled	–	Lancers, Swordsmen	26	4	4
Vassal, "Crusader" or mercenary men-at-arms	Knights	Heavily Armoured	Superior	Undrilled	–	Lancers, Swordsmen	23	4–6	0–6
	Knights	Heavily Armoured	Average	Drilled	–	Lancers, Swordsmen	21	4–6	
Turcopoles	Light horse	Unprotected	Average	Undrilled	Javelins	Light Spear	7	4–6	0–4
	Cavalry	Protected	Average	Undrilled	–	Light Spear, Swordsmen	9	4–6	
Serving brother or mercenary spearmen	Heavy Foot	Protected	Average	Drilled	–	Defensive Spearmen	7	4–6	0–6
Subject foot spearmen	Medium Foot	Protected	Average	Undrilled	–	Defensive Spearmen	6	4–6	
	Medium Foot	Protected	Poor	Undrilled	–	Defensive Spearmen	4	4–6	
German town militia spearmen	Heavy Foot	Protected	Poor	Drilled	–	Defensive Spearmen	5	4–6	
Serving brother or mercenary crossbowmen	Medium Foot	Protected	Average	Drilled	Crossbow	–	7	4–6	0–6
German town militia crossbowmen	Medium Foot	Protected	Poor	Drilled	Crossbow	–	5	4–6	
Vassal or "Crusader" crossbowmen	Medium Foot	Protected	Average	Undrilled	Crossbow	–	6	4–6	

Teutonic Knights, by Richard Scollins. Taken from Men-at-Arms 155: The Knights of Christ.

CATALAN COMPANY

The Catalan Grand Company, or Company of the Army of the Franks in Romania as it was officially called, was founded by the former Templar Roger de Flor after the Peace of Caltabellotta in 1302 made redundant the soldiers from Catalonia and Aragon who had been fighting against the French dynasty of Anjou in Sicily. This list covers the Company from its departure from Sicily until the fall of the state it founded in Greece to the Florentines.

The army was first hired in 1303 by the Byzantine Emperor Andronikos II Palaiologos to fight against the Turks. King Frederick III of Sicily supported the transfer as he was eager to get rid of them. Roger de Flor married the niece of Andronikos, daughter of the Tsar of Bulgaria, and was named Grand Duke, arriving at Constantinople with 1,500 horsemen and 4,000 almughavars, who were to be reinforced by 2,000 Greeks and 1,000 Alans supplied by the Byzantines. The combined force achieved its first successes at the battles of Tiraion and Aulax. After being reinforced with a further 200 knights and 1,000 almughavars under Bernat de Rocafort, the Company defeated the Turks again at Ania, and marched east to the Taurus Mountains. There it won a decisive victory against a larger Turkish army, neutralising the Turkish threat for some years.

The Company was then recalled to Constantinople to defeat the revolting Bulgars, who surrendered on hearing the news of its arrival. The Byzantines became afraid of the Company's rising power, especially after the arrival of a further 100 knights and 1,000 almughavars under Berenguer d'Entença. On 4 April 1305 De Flor and his bodyguard were assassinated (by the Alans) at a banquet ostensibly in their honour. The rest of the

Company was immediately attacked in Gallipoli by the Byzantine army under the Emperor's son Michael – he caused heavy casualties but failed to defeat them. The Company sent an embassy to challenge the Emperor, but these too were killed, along with all Catalans and Aragonese living in Constantinople. At the same time, Berenguer d'Entença decided to lead a punitive expedition by sea against the Empire with half of the Company's remaining men, but was captured by the Genoese and his men killed.

Only 206 horsemen and 1,256 foot soldiers under Bernat de Rocafort remained in Gallipoli. This encouraged Michael to order a final attack, only to be defeated and almost killed in the battle of Apros in July 1305. After this victory, what was to be called the "Catalan Vengeance" was unleashed: the Company devastated the regions of Thrace and Macedonia for the following two years, and increased its numbers again with Turcopoles formerly in Byzantine service, Ottoman mercenaries, Byzantine deserters, soldiers of fortune from all over Europe and more almughavars arrived from Sicily. Meanwhile, in July 1306, they had found, defeated and massacred the Alans who had assassinated their leaders the year before.

In 1307 Berenguer d'Entença, who had been released by the Genoese, joined the Company again, and some time later the Infante Ferran of Mallorca was sent by Frederick III of Sicily to lead the Company. However, his leadership was not accepted by Bernat de Rocafort. The internal disputes ended up with Entença killed, the Infante back in Sicily and Rocafort as sole commander. He offered the services of the Company to Charles de Valois to help in his claim to the Byzantine Empire, but in 1309, Thibault de Chepoy, Charles de Valois' deputy, ended the tyrannical rule of Rocafort, seizing him and sending him to Naples where he died the same year.

The Company then adopted a committee leadership and offered its service to Walter V de Brienne, Duke of Athens. Within a year it freed the Duchy of its enemies, only to be betrayed by the Duke who did not want to pay for its services. De Brienne, sure of the superiority of his knights over the almughavars, attacked them on 15 March 1311 in the Battle of Kephissos, but once again the almughavars won. De Brienne was killed and the Company seized control of the Duchy of Athens. Afterwards it expanded into Thessaly to create the Duchy of Neopatria and held both until 1388, when the remnants of the once powerful Catalan Grand Company were unable to resist the attack of the Florentines under Nerio I Acciaioli.

"DESPERTA FERRO"

This expression, meaning "awake the iron", was the war cry of the almughavars. It is linked to a ritual they repeated before every battle: They struck their swords and spearheads against their flints in order to produce sparks that should awake their weapons for the coming fight. Performed at night or dawn, the combination of the sparks, their cries and the sound of the metal hitting the stone must surely have had a terrifying effect on their enemies.

TROOP NOTES

Almughavars are described as lightly armoured and equipped with a couple of iron darts called "sagetes" or "escones", similar to the Roman pilum or the ancient Spanish soliferrum, a short sword or dagger, and a spear. Their fighting style relied on the effect of missiles combined with a fierce charge. Classification presents a problem – therefore we give a choice of classification. Drilled grading reflects the discipline and training gained after years of continuous service.

Muntaner, who was the Catalan Company's bookkeeper, details how much the Byzantines paid each "cavall armat" and each "cavall alforrat". The first were standard knights on eventually armoured horses, the second lighter knights on unarmoured horses riding a la jinete. In standard Catalan armies these "cavalls alforrats" usually fought mixed in the ranks of the heavier armoured knights, but their numbers in the Company were so high compared to those of the heavier knights that they had to fight on their own in a similar way to detached valets and other lighter knights of central European armies.

CATALAN COMPANY STARTER ARMY		
Commander-in-Chief	1	Field Commander
Sub-commanders	2	2 x Troop Commander
Cavalls alforrats	2 BGs	Each comprising 4 bases of cavalls alforrats: Superior, Armoured, Undrilled Cavalry – Lancers, Swordsmen
Turkish cavalry	1 BG	4 bases of Turkish cavalry: Average, Unprotected, Undrilled Light Horse – Bow, Swordsmen
Albanian cavalry	1 BG	4 bases of Albanian cavalry: Average, Unprotected, Undrilled Light Horse – Javelins, Light Spear, Swordsmen
Almughavars	3 BGs	Each comprising 8 bases of almughavars: Superior, Protected, Drilled Medium Foot – Offensive Spearmen
Greek archers	2 BGs	Each comprising 6 bases of Greek archers: Poor, Unprotected, Undrilled Light Foot – Bow
Camp	1	Unfortified camp
Total	9 BGs	Camp, 16 mounted bases, 36 foot bases, 3 commanders

BUILDING A CUSTOMISED LIST USING OUR ARMY POINTS

Choose an army based on the maxima and minima in the list below. The following special instructions apply to this army:

- Commanders should be depicted as cavalls armats.
- All Medium Foot almughavars must be classified the same.

CATALAN COMPANY

Territory Types: Agricultural, Developed, Hilly

C-in-C	Inspired Commander/Field Commander/Troop Commander						80/50/35		1
Sub-commanders	Field Commander						50		0–2
	Troop Commander						35		0–3

Troop name	Troop Type				Capabilities		Points per base	Bases per BG	Total bases
	Type	Armour	Quality	Training	Shooting	Close Combat			
Core Troops									
Cavalls armats	Knights	Heavily Armoured	Superior	Undrilled	–	Lancers, Swordsmen	23	4–6	0–6
Cavalls alforrats	Cavalry	Armoured	Superior	Undrilled	–	Lancers, Swordsmen	16	4–6	4–12 / 4–12
Almughavars	Medium Foot	Unprotected	Superior	Drilled	–	Offensive Spearmen	8	6–8	12–80
		Protected					10		
	Medium Foot	Unprotected	Superior	Drilled	–	Impact Foot, Swordsmen	8	6–8	
		Protected					10		
Almughavar skirmishers	Light Foot	Unprotected	Average	Drilled	Javelins	Light Spear	4	6–8	0–12
Crossbowmen	Medium Foot	Protected	Average	Drilled	Crossbow	–	7	6–8	0–12
	Light Foot	Unprotected	Average	Drilled	Crossbow	–	5	6–8	
Turks or Turcopoles — Only from 1305	Light horse	Unprotected	Average	Undrilled	Bow	Swordsmen	10	4–6	0–30 / 6–30
	Cavalry	Unprotected	Average	Undrilled	Bow	Swordsmen	10		
		Protected					11		
Albanians — Only from 1380	Light horse	Unprotected	Average	Undrilled	Javelins	Light Spear, Swordsmen	9	4–6	0–16
	Cavalry	Unprotected	Average	Undrilled	–	Light Spear, Swordsmen	8		
		Protected					9		
Optional Troops									
Greek archers	Medium Foot	Unprotected	Poor	Undrilled	Bow	–	3	6–8	0–12
	Light Foot	Unprotected	Poor	Undrilled	Bow	–	3	6–8	
Fortified camp							24		0–1
Allies									
Byzantine allies (Only before 1305) – Late Byzantine									
Alan allies (Only before 1305) – Later Alan – See Field of Glory Companion 4: *Swords and Scimitars: The Crusades*									

CATALAN COMPANY ALLIES

Allied commander		Field Commander/Troop Commander					40/25		1	
Troop name		Troop Type				Capabilities		Points per base	Bases per BG	Total bases
		Type	Armour	Quality	Training	Shooting	Close Combat			
Cavalls armats		Knights	Heavily Armoured	Superior	Undrilled	–	Lancers, Swordsmen	23	4–6	0–4
Cavalls alforrats		Cavalry	Armoured	Superior	Undrilled	–	Lancers, Swordsmen	16	4–6	
Almughavars		Medium Foot	Unprotected	Superior	Drilled	–	Offensive Spearmen	8	6–8	6–24
			Protected					10		
		Medium Foot	Unprotected	Superior	Drilled	–	Impact Foot, Swordsmen	8	6–8	
			Protected					10		
Almughavar skirmishers		Light Foot	Unprotected	Average	Drilled	Javelins	Light Spear	4	4–6	0–6
Crossbowmen		Medium Foot	Protected	Average	Drilled	Crossbow	–	7	4–6	0–6	0–8
		Light Foot	Unprotected	Average	Drilled	Crossbow	–	5	4–6	0–6	
Turks or Turcopoles	Only from 1305	Light horse	Unprotected	Average	Undrilled	Bow	Swordsmen	10		0–10	0–10
		Cavalry	Unprotected	Average	Undrilled	Bow	Swordsmen	10	4–6		
			Protected					11			
Albanians	Only from 1380	Light horse	Unprotected	Average	Undrilled	Javelins	Light Spear, Swordsmen	9		0–6	
		Cavalry	Unprotected	Average	Undrilled	–	Light Spear, Swordsmen	8	4–6		
			Protected					9			

MIDDLE HUNGARIAN

Under Charles I Robert (1308-1342), the first king of the Angevin dynasty, Hungary was successfully allied with Poland against the Holy Roman Empire, Austria and Bohemia. In the south, however, the reign was marked by a reduction in Hungarian power. Wallachia seceded in 1330, defeating the Hungarian army at the Battle of Posada the same year.

Under Charles's son Louis I (1342-1382), the kingdom expanded to include Bosnia and parts of Serbia and Bulgaria. There were also wars against Venice, Naples, the Ottoman Turks and the Golden Horde. In 1370 Louis inherited the throne of Poland and ruled the two kingdoms jointly until his death.

After his death Hungary went to the husband of his daughter Mary, the son of the Holy Roman Emperor Charles IV, Sigismund of the House of Luxembourg (1387-1437) and Poland to the husband of his daughter Jadwiga, Jogailo, Grand-Duke of Lithuania (1386-1434).

Cuman Horse Archer

Sigismund was also "King of the Romans" (the title of the Holy Roman Emperor elect prior to coronation by the Pope) from 1410 to 1433, and Holy Roman Emperor from 1433 until his death. He was titulary King of Bohemia from 1419. During his long reign he fought wars against Naples, the Ottoman Turks (including the Crusade of Nicopolis in 1396 which ended in disaster), Croatia and Bosnia, Venice and the Hussites of Bohemia. He was succeeded as King of Hungary by his son-in-law the Duke of Austria, Albrecht of Habsburg (1437-1439).

After the latter's death, the throne went to the Polish King Władysław III (1440-1444), passing over the claim of Albrecht's son Ladislaus V Posthumus (born after Albrecht's death) who did not ascend the throne until Władysław's death at the Battle of Varna against the Ottomans.

This list covers Hungarian armies from 1308 to 1440.

TROOP NOTES

Classification of Szeklers presents some difficulty, so we have given a choice of interpretations.

MIDDLE HUNGARIAN STARTER ARMY		
Commander-in-Chief	1	Field Commander
Sub-commanders	2	2 x Troop Commander
Hungarian nobles	2 BGs	Each comprising 4 bases of Hungarian nobles: Superior, Heavily Armoured, Undrilled Knights – Lancers, Swordsmen
Szeklers	2 BGs	Each comprising 4 bases of szeklers: Superior, Protected, Undrilled Cavalry – Bow*, Light Spear, Swordsmen
Hungarian horse archers	2 BGs	Each comprising 4 bases of Hungarian horse archers: Average, Unprotected, Undrilled Light Horse – Bow
Cuman horse archers	2 BGs	Each comprising 4 bases of Cuman horse archers: Average, Unprotected, Undrilled Light Horse – Bow, Swordsmen
Foot archers	1 BG	8 bases of foot archers: Average, Unprotected, Undrilled Light Foot – Bow
Camp	1	Unfortified camp
Total	9 BGs	Camp, 32 mounted bases, 8 foot bases, 3 commanders

BUILDING A CUSTOMISED LIST USING OUR ARMY POINTS

Choose an army based on the maxima and minima in the list below. The following special instructions apply to this army:

- Commanders should be depicted as nobles or mercenary men-at-arms.

Foot Archer

MIDDLE HUNGARIAN

Territory Types: Agricultural, Hilly

C-in-C	Inspired Commander/Field Commander/Troop Commander						80/50/35		1	
Sub-commanders	Field Commander						50		0–2	
	Troop Commander						35		0–3	

Troop name	Troop Type				Capabilities		Points per base	Bases per BG	Total bases	
	Type	Armour	Quality	Training	Shooting	Close Combat				
Core Troops										
Hungarian nobles	Knights	Heavily Armoured	Superior	Undrilled	–	Lancers, Swordsmen	23	4–6	4–12	
Mercenary men-at-arms	Knights	Heavily Armoured	Average	Drilled	–	Lancers, Swordsmen	21	4–6		
Hungarian, Cuman, Jazyges or Ruthenian horse archers	Light horse	Unprotected	Average	Undrilled	Bow	–	8	4–6	12–36	
	Light horse	Unprotected	Average	Undrilled	Bow	Swordsmen	10	4–6		
Szeklers	Light Horse	Unprotected	Superior	Undrilled	Bow	Swordsmen	12	4–6	0–18	0–18
			Average				10			
	Light Horse	Unprotected	Superior	Undrilled	Bow	Light Spear, Swordsmen	13			
			Average				11			
	Cavalry	Unprotected	Superior	Undrilled	Bow	Swordsmen	12			
		Unprotected	Average				10			
		Protected	Superior				14			
		Protected	Average				11			
	Cavalry	Unprotected	Superior	Undrilled	Bow*	Light Spear, Swordsmen	12			
		Unprotected	Average				10			
		Protected	Superior				14			
		Protected	Average				11			
	Cavalry	Armoured	Superior	Undrilled	Bow*	Light Spear, Swordsmen	18	4–6	0–6	
Optional Troops										
Tatars	Light Horse	Unprotected	Average	Undrilled	Bow	Swordsmen	10	4–6	0–6	
	Cavalry	Unprotected	Average	Undrilled	Bow	Swordsmen	10			
		Protected					11			
Spearmen	Heavy Foot	Protected	Average	Undrilled	–	Defensive Spearmen	6	6–8	0–12	
			Poor				4			
Foot archers	Medium Foot	Unprotected	Average	Undrilled	Bow	–	5	6–8	0–24	0–24
			Poor				3			
	Light Foot	Unprotected	Average	Undrilled	Bow	–	5	6–8		
			Poor				3			
Shielded Bosnian foot archers	Medium Foot	Protected	Average	Undrilled	Bow	–	6	6–8	0–12	
Fortified camp							24		0–1	
Allies										
Moldavian allies										
Polish allies – Later Polish										
Wallachian allies										
Special Campaigns										
Crusade of Nicopolis 1396										
Crusader allied general	Troop Commander						25		1	
Crusader knights	Knights	Heavily Armoured	Superior	Undrilled	–	Lancers, Swordsmen	23	4–6	4–16	

Wallachian allies are compulsory, but cannot total more than 12 bases.

MIDDLE HUNGARIAN ALLIES

Allied commander	Field Commander/Troop Commander						40/25	1	
	Troop Type				Capabilities		Points per base	Bases per BG	Total bases
Troop name	Type	Armour	Quality	Training	Shooting	Close Combat			
Hungarian nobles	Knights	Heavily Armoured	Superior	Undrilled	–	Lancers, Swordsmen	23	4	0–4
Mercenary men-at-arms	Knights	Heavily Armoured	Average	Drilled	–	Lancers, Swordsmen	21	4	
Hungarian, Cuman, Jazyges or Ruthenian horse archers	Light horse	Unprotected	Average	Undrilled	Bow	–	8	4–6	4–12
	Light horse	Unprotected	Average	Undrilled	Bow	Swordsmen	10	4–6	
Szeklers	Light Horse	Unprotected	Superior	Undrilled	Bow	Swordsmen	12	4–6	0–6
			Average				10		
	Light Horse	Unprotected	Superior	Undrilled	Bow	Light Spear, Swordsmen	13		
			Average				11		
	Cavalry	Unprotected	Superior	Undrilled	Bow	Swordsmen	12		
		Unprotected	Average				10		
		Protected	Superior				14		
		Protected	Average				11		
	Cavalry	Unprotected	Superior	Undrilled	Bow*	Light Spear, Swordsmen	12		
		Unprotected	Average				10		
		Protected	Superior				14		
		Protected	Average				11		
Foot archers	Medium Foot	Unprotected	Average	Undrilled	Bow	–	5	6–8	0–8
			Poor				3		
	Light Foot	Unprotected	Average	Undrilled	Bow	–	5	6–8	
			Poor				3		

Hungarian Cavalry, by Angus McBride. Taken from Men-at-Arms 195:
Hungary and the fall of Eastern Europe 1000–1568.

MOLDAVIAN OR WALLACHIAN

This list covers the armies of the Romanian principalities of Moldavia and Wallachia from their gaining independence from Hungary in 1359 AD and 1330 respectively, until 1500. Moldavia was nominally a Polish-Lithuanian vassal from 1395. Although Wallachia was tributary to the Ottomans from 1392, and a vassal state from 1476, it nevertheless retained autonomy.

VLAD THE IMPALER

Vlad the Impaler (Vlad III Țepeș) ruled as Prince (Voivode) of Wallachia in 1448, from 1456–1462, and again in 1476 after a long period of captivity in Hungary. His nickname of Dracula (Drăculea – "Son of the Dragon") derives from his father Vlad II Dracul's cognomen as a member of the Order of the Dragon. This was a chivalric order founded by King Sigismund of Hungary and dedicated to defending Christianity against the Turks.

Once in power, Vlad eliminated his political rivals, principally by impalement, suppressing the power of the boyars and relying on the loyalty of the free peasantry.

In 1459 he stopped paying tribute to the Turks and made an alliance with Matthias Corvinus, King of Hungary. From 1461–62 he made a savage raid into Turkish territory. In response, the Ottoman Sultan Mehmed II invaded Wallachia. Outnumbered 3 to 1, Vlad was unable to offer open battle, instead engaging in a scorched earth policy and a guerrilla

Crossbowman

terror campaign of raids and ambushes. Just before the Turks reached the Wallachian capital, Târgoviște, Vlad made a night attack on the Ottoman camp with up to 10,000 men, with the aim of killing the Sultan in his tent. The Sultan survived, but up to 15,000 Turks were killed. Outside Târgoviște, the Turks found 20,000 decomposed Turkish corpses impaled on a forest of stakes. The next day Mehmed began the retreat. However, before leaving Wallachia altogether, he set up Vlad's pro-Turkish brother Radu the Handsome as a rival for power. Many Wallachians, tired of Vlad's reign of terror, soon defected to Radu and Vlad was forced to flee to

Eastern Europe, c.1386. Taken from Campaign 122: Tannenberg 1410.

join his ally King Matthias. Contrary to his expectations, however, the latter imprisoned him and recognised Radu as Voivode. Vlad remained in captivity for 12 years.

In 1476, with his brother Radu dead, and a new rival, Basarab Laiotă, on the throne, Vlad reinvaded Wallachia with a force of Transylvanians, Moldavians and Wallachians. After his allies had returned home, however, his position was weak, and he was killed in battle against Basarab and his Turkish allies two months after his return to Wallachia.

WALLACHIAN STARTER ARMY

Commander-in-Chief	1	Inspired Commander (Vlad III Ţepeş)
Sub-commanders	2	2 x Troop Commander
Nobles	2 BGs	Each comprising 4 bases of nobles: Superior, Armoured, Undrilled Cavalry – Bow*, Light Spear, Swordsmen
Cavalry	4 BGs	Each comprising 4 bases of cavalry: Average, Unprotected, Undrilled Light Horse – Bow, Light Spear, Swordsmen
Curteni archers	1 BG	8 bases of Curteni archers: Average, Protected, Undrilled Medium Foot – Bow
Foot archers	2 BGs	Each comprising 8 bases of foot archers: Average, Unprotected, Undrilled Light Foot – Bow
Camp	1	Unfortified camp
Total	9 BGs	Camp, 24 mounted bases, 24 foot bases, 3 commanders

BUILDING A CUSTOMISED LIST USING OUR ARMY POINTS

Choose an army based on the maxima and minima in the list below. The following special instructions apply to this army:

- Commanders should be depicted as nobles.

- Only one allied contingent can be used.

Handgunner

MOLDAVIAN OR WALLACHIAN

Territory Types: Agricultural, Hilly, Woodlands, Mountains

C-in-C		Inspired Commander/Field Commander/Troop Commander					80/50/35	1	
Sub-commanders		Field Commander					50	0–2	
		Troop Commander					35	0–3	
Troop name		**Troop Type**				**Capabilities**	**Points per base**	**Bases per BG**	**Total bases**
		Type	Armour	Quality	Training	Shooting	Close Combat		

Core Troops									
Nobles	Any	Cavalry	Armoured	Superior	Undrilled	Bow*	Light Spear, Swordsmen	18	4–6	4–12
	Only Moldavians from 1400	Knights	Armoured	Superior	Undrilled	–	Lancers, Swordsmen	20	4–6	
Cavalry		Light Horse	Unprotected	Superior	Undrilled	Bow	Light Spear, Swordsmen	13		8–32
				Average				11	4–6	
		Cavalry	Unprotected	Superior	Undrilled	Bow*	Light Spear, Swordsmen	12		
			Unprotected	Average				10		
			Protected	Superior				14		
			Protected	Average				11		
Curteni archers		Medium Foot	Protected	Average	Undrilled	Bow	–	6	6–8	0–18
Other archers		Medium Foot	Unprotected	Average	Undrilled	Bow	–	5		12–72
				Poor				3	6–8	
		Light Foot	Unprotected	Average	Undrilled	Bow	–	5		
				Poor				3		

Optional Troops									
Mercenary men-at-arms	Only Wallachians	Knights	Heavily Armoured	Average	Drilled	–	Lancers, Swordsmen	21	4	0–4
Voynuks		Heavy Foot	Armoured	Average	Undrilled	–	Heavy Weapon	9	4–6	0–6
Peasants with assorted weapons		Medium Foot	Unprotected	Average	Undrilled	–	Light Spear	4	6–8	0–16
		Mob	Unprotected	Poor	Undrilled	–	–	2	8–12	
Crossbowmen		Light Foot	Unprotected	Average	Undrilled	Crossbow	–	5	4	0–4
Handgunners	Only from 1430	Light Foot	Unprotected	Average	Undrilled	Firearm	–	4	4	0–4
Bombards	Only from 1400	Heavy Guns	–	Average	Undrilled	–	–	20	2	0–2
Field Fortifications	Wallachians	FF						3		0–12
	Moldavians									0–32
Fortified camp								24		0–1

Allies
Hungarian allies – Middle Hungarian or Later Hungarian
Ottoman allies – Later Ottoman Turkish
Only Moldavians
Crimean Tatar allies – Tatar
Polish allies – Later Polish
Only Wallachians
Moldavian allies – Moldavian or Wallachian

MOLDAVIAN OR WALLACHIAN

MOLDAVIAN OR WALLACHIAN ALLIES

Allied commander		Field Commander/Troop Commander					40/25	1	
Troop name		Troop Type				Capabilities		Points per base	Bases per BG	Total bases
		Type	Armour	Quality	Training	Shooting	Close Combat			
Nobles	Any	Cavalry	Armoured	Superior	Undrilled	Bow*	Light Spear, Swordsmen	18	4	0–4
	Only Moldavians from 1400	Knights	Armoured	Superior	Undrilled	–	Lancers, Swordsmen	20	4	
Cavalry		Light Horse	Unprotected	Superior	Undrilled	Bow	Light Spear, Swordsmen	13	4–6	4–12
				Average				11		
		Cavalry	Unprotected	Superior	Undrilled	Bow*	Light Spear, Swordsmen	12		
			Unprotected	Average				10		
			Protected	Superior				14		
			Protected	Average				11		
Curteni archers		Medium Foot	Protected	Average	Undrilled	Bow	–	6	6–8	0–8
Other archers		Medium Foot	Unprotected	Average	Undrilled	Bow	–	5	6–8	0–18
				Poor				3		
		Light Foot	Unprotected	Average	Undrilled	Bow	–	5		
				Poor				3		

Moldavian light cavalry and Wallachian infantry, c.1500, by Angus McBride. Taken from Men-at-Arms 195: Hungary and the fall of Eastern Europe 1000–1568.

ALBANIAN

This list covers Albanian armies from 1356-1358, when local rulers asserted their independence from Serbia and the Angevins, until conquest by the Ottomans in 1430, then from the rebellion of Scanderbeg in 1443 until the collapse of Albanian resistance in 1478.

ALBANIAN STARTER ARMY		
Commander-in-Chief	1	Inspired Commander (Scanderbeg)
Sub-commanders	2	2 x Troop Commander
Mercenary men-at-arms	1 BG	4 bases of mercenary men-at-arms: Average, Heavily Armoured, Drilled Knights – Lancers, Swordsmen
Veteran cavalry	2 BGs	Each comprising 4 bases of veteran cavalry: Superior, Protected, Undrilled Cavalry – Light Spear, Swordsmen
Other cavalry	5 BGs	Each comprising 4 bases of other cavalry: Average, Unprotected, Undrilled Light Horse – Javelins, Light Spear, Swordsmen
Archers	3 BGs	Each comprising 6 bases of archers: Average, Unprotected, Undrilled Light Foot – Bow
Camp	1	Unfortified camp
Total	11 BGs	Camp, 32 mounted bases, 18 foot bases, 3 commanders

BUILDING A CUSTOMISED LIST USING OUR ARMY POINTS

Choose an army based on the maxima and minima in the list below. The following special instructions apply to this army:

- Commanders should be depicted as cavalry.
- The minimum marked * applies if any Venetian, Neapolitan or Neapolitan supplied troops are used.
- A Venetian allied commander can only command Venetian troops, and must command all such troops.
- A Neapolitan allied commander can only command Neapolitan or Neapolitan supplied troops, and must command all such troops.
- Ottoman allies represent Ottoman forces supporting anti-Scanderbeg factions. They cannot include Qapu Khalqi cavalry or Janissaries.

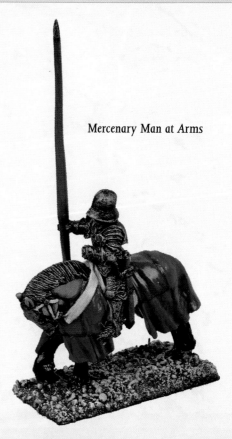

Mercenary Man at Arms

Albanian Mercenary, by Angus McBride. Taken from Men-at-Arms 287: Byzantine Armies, AD 1118–1461.

ALBANIAN

Territory Types: Hilly, Mountains

C-in-C		Inspired Commander/Field Commander/Troop Commander					80/50/35		1	
Sub-commanders		Field Commander					50		0–2	
		Troop Commander					35		0–3	
Troop name		Troop Type				Capabilities		Points per base	Bases per BG	Total bases
		Type	Armour	Quality	Training	Shooting	Close Combat			
Core Troops										
Veteran cavalry		Light Horse	Unprotected	Superior	Undrilled	Javelins	Light Spear, Swordsmen	11	4–6	4–18
		Cavalry	Unprotected	Superior	Undrilled	–	Light Spear, Swordsmen	10	4–6	
			Protected					12		
Other cavalry		Light Horse	Unprotected	Average	Undrilled	Javelins	Light Spear, Swordsmen	9	4–6	12–56
		Cavalry	Unprotected	Average	Undrilled	–	Light Spear, Swordsmen	8	4–6	
			Protected					9		
Mounted crossbowmen		Light Horse	Unprotected	Average	Undrilled	Crossbow	–	7	4–6	0–12
Archers		Medium Foot	Unprotected	Average	Undrilled	Bow	–	5	6–8	8–36
		Light Foot	Unprotected	Average	Undrilled	Bow	–	5		
Optional Troops										
Mercenary men-at-arms	Only from 1450	Knights	Heavily Armoured	Average	Drilled	–	Lancers, Swordsmen	21	4	0–4
Crossbowmen		Light Foot	Unprotected	Average	Undrilled	Crossbow	–	5	6–8	0–16
		Medium Foot	Unprotected	Average	Undrilled	Crossbow	–	5	6–8	0–16
		Medium Foot	Protected	Average	Undrilled	Crossbow	–	6	6–8	0–8
Halberdiers		Heavy Foot	Armoured	Average	Undrilled	–	Heavy Weapon	9	4–6	0–6
			Protected					7		
Javelinmen		Light Foot	Unprotected	Average	Undrilled	Javelins	Light Spear	4	6–8	0–12
		Medium Foot	Protected	Average	Undrilled	–	Light Spear	5	6–8	
Handgunners	Only from 1440	Light Foot	Unprotected	Average	Undrilled	Firearm	–	4	4	0–4
Peasant levy		Mob	Unprotected	Poor	Undrilled	–	–	2	6–8	0–8
Light guns		Light Artillery	–	Average	Undrilled	Light Artillery	–	15	2	0–2
Bombards		Heavy Artillery	–	Average	Undrilled	Heavy Artillery	–	20	2	
Venetian or Neapolitan allied commander		Field Commander/Troop Commander						40/25		*1
Venetian or Neapolitan mercenary men-at-arms	Venetians only before 1400, Neapolitans only from 1450	Knights	Heavily Armoured	Average	Drilled	–	Lancers, Swordsmen	21	4	0–4
Venetian, Neapolitan or Neapolitan supplied Catalan crossbowmen		Medium Foot	Protected	Average	Drilled	Crossbow	–	7	4	0–4
		Light Foot	Unprotected	Average	Drilled or Undrilled	Crossbow	–	5	4	
Neapolitan handgunners		Light Foot	Unprotected	Average	Drilled	Firearm	–	4	4	0–4
Neapolitan archers		Light Foot	Unprotected	Average	Drilled	Bow	–	5	4	0–4
Allies										

Ottoman allies – Later Ottoman Turkish

ALBANIAN ALLIES								
Allied commander	Field Commander/Troop Commander					40/25	1	
Troop name	Troop Type				Capabilities		Points per base	Bases per BG	Total bases
	Type	Armour	Quality	Training	Shooting	Close Combat			
Veteran cavalry	Light Horse	Unprotected	Superior	Undrilled	Javelins	Light Spear, Swordsmen	11	4–6	0–6
	Cavalry	Unprotected	Superior	Undrilled	–	Light Spear, Swordsmen	10	4–6	
		Protected					12		
Other cavalry	Light Horse	Unprotected	Average	Undrilled	Javelins	Light Spear, Swordsmen	9	4–6	4–12
	Cavalry	Unprotected	Average	Undrilled	–	Light Spear, Swordsmen	8	4–6	
		Protected					9		
Mounted crossbowmen	Light Horse	Unprotected	Average	Undrilled	Crossbow	–	7	4	0–4
Archers	Medium Foot	Unprotected	Average	Undrilled	Bow	–	5	6–8	0–12
	Light Foot	Unprotected	Average	Undrilled	Bow	–	5		

TIMURID, BLACK SHEEP TURCOMAN OR WHITE SHEEP TURCOMAN

This list covers the Timurids from 1360 AD until 1500, the Black Sheep Turcomans (Qara-Qoyunlu) from 1378 until 1469, and the White Sheep Turcomans (Aq-Qoyunlu) from 1402 until 1500.

TIMUR

Tīmūr bin Taraghay Barlas, known in the West as Tamerlane (Timur the Lame), was born in Transoxiana of Turco-Mongolian descent. From about 1360 he gained prominence as a warlord, soon relegating the Khan of Chagatai to the status of a figurehead, and making his capital at Samarkand (in modern Uzbekistan). He never actually claimed the title of Khan for himself. During the course of his many conquests, many centres of civilization were destroyed, and it has been estimated that up to 17 million people may have been slaughtered. He built pyramids of the skulls of his opponents, 70,000 outside Isfahan alone – but built little more permanent. Though a military genius, he tended not to consolidate his conquests, often needing to reconquer the

same region several times. Though he thought of himself as a Mongol and as a ghazi of Islam, he dealt an ultimately fatal blow to the Mongol Golden Horde and most of his wars were against Muslim states. He decisively defeated the Ottoman Turks at Ankara in 1402, but contented himself with re-establishing the independent Anatolian emirates the Ottomans had conquered, thus giving the Ottomans a reprieve which allowed them to recover and eventually gain a huge empire.

Timur's empire included modern Syria, Iraq, Iran, Kazakhstan, Afghanistan, Azerbaijan, Georgia, Turkmenistan, Uzbekistan, Kyrgyzstan, Pakistan, NW India, and even approached China.

He fell sick and died in 1405 while campaigning against the Ming Chinese.

He was succeeded by his son Shah Rukh (1405–1447) who secured Persia and Transoxiana for the Timurid Empire, though its western territories were lost to the Black Sheep Turcomans. In the early 16th century, the main Timurid centres of Samarkand and Herat were

Timurid Cavalry, c. 1400, by Angus McBride. Taken from Men-at-Arms 222: The Age of Tamerlane.

conquered by the Uzbeks, but the Timurid ruler of Fergana, Bābur, a direct descendant of Timur, invaded India and founded the Mughal Empire which lasted until 1857.

BLACK SHEEP TURCOMANS

The Black Sheep Turcomans (Qara Qoyunlu) held land in eastern modern Turkey and Armenia from the mid 14th century, extending into Azerbaijan by the end of the century. In 1400 they were defeated by Timur and their ruler, Qara Yusuf, fled into exile. He returned, however, and by 1406 had recaptured Tabriz after defeating the Timurids at Nakhichevan. In 1410, he took Baghdad from the Jalayrids. At their height the Black Sheep Turcomans ruled modern Armenia, Azerbaijan, the Southern

Caucasus and Iraq. In 1467, however, they were defeated by the White Sheep Turcomans, who took over their territory.

WHITE SHEEP TURCOMANS

The White Sheep Turcomans (Aq Qoyunlu) were granted lands in eastern modern Turkey by Timur following his defeat of the Ottomans at Ankara in 1402. In 1467, under Uzun Hasan, they defeated the Black Sheep Turcomans and took over their territory. At their height they ruled modern eastern Turkey, Armenia, Azerbaijan, northern Iraq and western Iran. In 1473, however, they were defeated by the Ottomans at Tercan, losing their territories in Turkey. After 1490 the dynasty collapsed into civil war. They were conquered by the Safavids by 1508.

TIMURID STARTER ARMY		
Commander-in-Chief	1	Inspired Commander (Timur)
Sub-commanders	2	2 x Troop Commander
Drilled cavalry	3 BGs	Each comprising 4 bases of drilled cavalry: Superior, Armoured, Drilled Cavalry – Bow, Swordsmen
Other Georgian, Persian or Turcoman heavy cavalry	1 BG	4 bases of other heavy cavalry: Superior, Armoured, Undrilled Cavalry – Bow, Swordsmen
Turcoman tribal cavalry	2 BGs	Each comprising 4 bases of Turcoman tribal cavalry: Average, Unprotected, Undrilled Light Horse – Bow, Swordsmen
Well equipped foot archers	1 BG	8 bases of well equipped foot archers: Average, Protected, Drilled, Medium Foot – Bow
Women disguised as warriors to protect camp	1 BG	6 bases of disguised women: Poor, Unprotected, Undrilled Mob – no capabilities
Camp	1	Unfortified camp
Total	8 BGs	Camp, 24 mounted bases, 14 foot bases, 3 commanders

BUILDING A CUSTOMISED LIST USING OUR ARMY POINTS

Choose an army based on the maxima and minima in the list below. The following special instructions apply to this army:

- Commanders should be depicted as drilled cavalry.
- Drilled cavalry can always dismount as Superior, Armoured, Drilled Medium Foot – Bow, Swordsmen.

TIMURID, BLACK SHEEP TURCOMAN OR WHITE SHEEP TURCOMAN

Territory Types: Agricultural, Steppes								
C-in-C	Inspired Commander/Field Commander/Troop Commander					80/50/35	1	
Sub-commanders	Field Commander					50	0–2	
	Troop Commander					35	0–3	
Troop name	Troop Type				Capabilities		Points per base	Bases per BG	Total bases
	Type	Armour	Quality	Training	Shooting	Close Combat			
Core Troops									
Drilled cavalry	Cavalry	Armoured	Superior	Drilled	Bow	Swordsmen	19	4–6	12–30
Optional Troops									
Other Georgian, Persian or Turcoman heavy cavalry	Cavalry	Armoured	Superior	Undrilled	Bow	Swordsmen	18	4–6	0–12
			Average				14		
Turcoman tribal cavalry	Light Horse	Unprotected	Average	Undrilled	Bow	Swordsmen	10	4–6	0–18
	Cavalry	Unprotected	Average	Undrilled	Bow	Swordsmen	10		
		Protected					11		
Kurdish cavalry	Only Black or White Sheep	Cavalry	Armoured	Superior	Undrilled	–	Lancers, Swordsmen	16	4–6	0–12
			Armoured	Average				12		
			Protected	Superior				12		
			Protected	Average				9		
Well equipped foot archers	Medium Foot	Protected	Average	Drilled	Bow	–	7	6–8	0–12
Other foot archers	Medium Foot	Unprotected	Average	Undrilled	Bow	–	5	6–8	0–16
			Poor				3		
Hillmen	Medium Foot	Protected	Average	Undrilled	–	Light Spear	5	6–8	0–8
Handgunners	Only from 1470	Light foot	Unprotected	Average	Undrilled	Firearm	–	4	4	0–4
Women disguised as warriors to protect camp	Mob	Unprotected	Poor	Undrilled	–	–	2	6–8	0–8
Elephants	Only Timurids	Elephants	–	Average	Undrilled	–	–	25	2	0–4
Stone throwers or heavy guns	Heavy Artillery	–	Average	Undrilled	Heavy Artillery	–	20	2	0–2
Fortified camp							24		0–1
Allies									

Only Timurids

Black Sheep or White Sheep Turcoman allies

Uzbek allies – Later Tribal Mongol (see page 71)

Only White Sheep

Georgian allies – See Field of Glory Companion 4: *Swords and Scimitars: The Crusades*

Anatolian Turcoman allies

Turcoman tribesman, Turcoman cavalryman and Georgian heavy cavalryman, by Angus McBride. Taken from Men-at-Arms 222: The Age of Tamerlane.

BLACK SHEEP TURCOMAN OR WHITE SHEEP TURCOMAN ALLIES

Allied commander		Field Commander/Troop Commander						40/25	1	
Troop name		Troop Type				Capabilities		Points per base	Bases per BG	Total bases
		Type	Armour	Quality	Training	Shooting	Close Combat			
Drilled cavalry		Cavalry	Armoured	Superior	Drilled	Bow	Swordsmen	19	4–6	4–8
Other Georgian, Persian or Turcoman heavy cavalry		Cavalry	Armoured	Superior	Undrilled	Bow	Swordsmen	18	4	0–4
Turcoman tribal cavalry		Light Horse	Unprotected	Average	Undrilled	Bow	Swordsmen	10	4–6	0–6
		Cavalry	Unprotected	Average	Undrilled	Bow	Swordsmen	10		
			Protected					11		
Kurdish cavalry	Only Black or White Sheep	Cavalry	Armoured	Superior	Undrilled	–	Lancers, Swordsmen	16	4	0–4
			Armoured	Average				12		
			Protected	Superior				12		
			Protected	Average				9		
Well equipped foot archers		Medium Foot	Protected	Average	Drilled	Bow	–	7	6–8	0–8
Other foot archers		Medium Foot	Unprotected	Average	Undrilled	Bow	–	5	6–8	
				Poor				3		

HUSSITE

This list covers Hussite armies from Jan Žižka's revolt in 1419 until the peace of Olomouc in 1479.

On 6 July 1415 the Council of Constance, with the complicity of King Sigismund (King of Hungary and "King of the Romans"), executed the Bohemian religious reformer Jan Hus. Following this, anti-Catholic unrest began to grow in Bohemia. Anti-Hussite reaction was encouraged by King Wenceslaus of Bohemia, Sigismund's brother. On 30 July 1419 in Prague, anti-Hussites threw stones at a Hussite procession from the windows of the town-hall. In response, the Hussites, led by Jan Žižka, threw the burgomeister and several town-councillors from the windows (the "First Defenestration of Prague"), whereupon the mob killed them. King Wenceslaus suffered a stroke on hearing the news, and died soon after.

Following the childless King's death, Sigismund claimed the throne of Bohemia and severe fighting broke out between Catholic and Hussite factions. On 17 March 1420, Pope Martin V issued a bull proclaiming a crusade "for the destruction of the Wycliffites, Hussites and all other heretics in Bohemia". The first pitched battle occurred on 25 March 1420 at Sudoměř. 400 Hussites with 12 wagons defeated an assault by 2,000 dismounted royalist cavalry.

Sigismund then invaded with a large army of crusaders from Germany and all over Europe, but was decisively defeated by the Hussites near the village of Pankrác on 1st November 1420. 12,000 Hussites defeated a head on attack by 18,000 crusaders.

In 1421 another large army of crusaders invaded. Sigismund joined them later in the year. At Kutna Hora in December 1421, Žižka's outnumbered forces broke through Sigismund's army and escaped. In January 1422 Sigismund's forces were defeated at Neovidy, Habry and Nemecky Brod.

In 1423, civil war broke out between the moderate Utraquist faction of the Hussites and the more extreme Taborites. The Taborites, under Žižka, defeated the Utraquists, under Čeněk of Wartenberg, at Horic. In 1424, there was further civil strife between Žižka's Orebite faction (a less extreme splinter group of the Taborites) and the Utraquist City of Prague. The Prague army was defeated at Malesov. Reconciled, the combined forces of the Orebites, Utraquists and their Polish allies invaded Moravia, where a majority of the population supported their creed. However, following Žižka's death from the plague, they withdrew.

The Taborites then elected Prokop "the Bald" as their leader, the Orebites (or "Orphans" as they now called themselves) elected Prokop "the Lesser". From 1425 to 1426 Hussite forces campaigned in Silesia and Saxony. The Pope declared a new crusade. On 16th June 1426 the combined Taborite, Orebite and Utraquist forces defeated the crusaders at Ústí nad Labem (Aussig). In 1427 a further crusader army was routed without a shot fired at Meiss. For the next few years the Hussites conducted repeated forays into Hungary, Silesia, Lusatia, Meissen and Saxony. In 1431, at Domazlice (Taus), another crusader army took flight on seeing the Hussite banners and hearing their battle hymns.

Having lost hope of ever suppressing the Hussites, the Emperor and the Church offered to accept the 4 principal demands of the Hussites and legalise the ownership of lands seized from the church, under the terms of the Concordat of Basle. The Taborites and Orebites refused to accept the treaty, but In 1434, at Cesky Brod

Hussite cavalry

(Lipany), were defeated by combined Utraquist and Catholic forces. Following this, Bohemia accepted Sigismund as its King and the wars ended.

In 1462 the Church attempted to repudiate the Concordat of Basle and reimpose Catholicism. This caused a resumption of the Hussite wars, which lasted until the peace of Olomouc in 1479.

BATTLE WAGONS

The Hussites made systematic use of battle wagons. Their army formed up inside a wagon-fortress consisting of wagons protected by wooden hoardings usually drawn up in a rectangle with the wagons joined together by chains. Accounts of the standard wagon crew vary, but according to the "Hodětin Ordinance" it consisted of 20 men: 2 drivers, 2 handgunners, 6 crossbowmen, 4 flailmen, 4 halberdiers and 2 pavisiers. Other sources give a crew of 10 men, but with similar proportions. The handgunners and crossbowmen shot from inside the wagons, while the flailmen and halberdiers defended the gaps between the wagons. The enemy would be goaded into attacking by artillery fire. After the initial enemy assault was repulsed, Hussite cavalry and infantry would counterattack to complete the victory.

Battle Wagon and Bohemian Nobles

HUSSITE STARTER ARMY		
Commander-in-Chief	1	Inspired Commander (Jan Žižka)
Sub-commanders	2	2 x Troop Commander
Battle wagons	4 BGs	Each comprising 2 bases of battle wagons: Average, Undrilled Battle Wagons – Crossbow, Heavy Weapon
Hussite cavalry	2 BGs	Each comprising 4 bases of Hussite cavalry: Superior, Armoured, Drilled Cavalry – Lancers, Swordsmen
Mounted crossbowmen	1 BG	4 bases of mounted crossbowmen: Average, Unprotected, Drilled Light Horse – Crossbow
Separately deployed polearmsmen	1 BG	8 bases of polearmsmen: Superior, Armoured, Undrilled, Heavy Foot – Heavy Weapon
Camp	1	Unfortified camp
Total	8 BGs	Camp, 12 mounted bases, 16 foot bases, 3 commanders

BUILDING A CUSTOMISED LIST USING OUR ARMY POINTS

Choose an army based on the maxima and minima in the list below. The following special instructions apply to this army:

- Commanders should be depicted as Hussite cavalry or Bohemian nobles.

Battle Wagon

HUSSITE								
Territory Types: Agricultural, Hilly								
C-in-C	Inspired Commander/Field Commander/Troop Commander						80/50/35	1
Sub-commanders	Field Commander						50	0–2
	Troop Commander						35	0–3
Troop name	Troop Type				Capabilities		Points per base	Bases per BG	Total bases
	Type	Armour	Quality	Training	Shooting	Close Combat			
Core Troops									
Hussite cavalry	Cavalry	Armoured	Superior	Drilled	–	Lancers, Swordsmen	17	4–6	0–8
			Average				13		
Battle wagons and crew	Battle Wagons	–	Average	Undrilled	Crossbow	Heavy Weapon	23	2–4	8–40
Optional Troops									
Bohemian nobles	Knights	Heavily Armoured	Superior	Undrilled	–	Lancers, Swordsmen	23	4	0–8
Mounted crossbowmen	Light Horse	Unprotected	Average	Drilled	Crossbow	–	7	4	0–4
Separately deployed polearmsmen	Heavy Foot	Protected	Average	Undrilled	–	Heavy Weapon	7	6–8	0–16
		Protected	Average	Drilled			8		
		Protected	Superior	Undrilled			9		
		Protected	Superior	Drilled			10		
		Armoured	Average	Undrilled			9		
		Armoured	Average	Drilled			10		
		Armoured	Superior	Undrilled			12		
		Armoured	Superior	Drilled			13		
Light guns	Light Artillery	–	Average	Undrilled	Light Artillery	–	15	2	0–8
	Battle Wagons	–	Average	Undrilled	Light Artillery	Heavy Weapon	26		
Heavy guns	Heavy Artillery	–	Average	Undrilled	Heavy Artillery	–	20	2	0–2
Entrenchments to protect artillery when not on wagons	FF						3		0–24
Fortified camp							24		0–1
Allies									
Polish allies – Later Polish									

HUSSITE ALLIES								
Allied commander	Field Commander/Troop Commander						40/25	1
Troop name	Troop Type				Capabilities		Points per base	Bases per BG	Total bases
	Type	Armour	Quality	Training	Shooting	Close Combat			
Hussite cavalry	Cavalry	Armoured	Superior	Drilled	–	Lancers, Swordsmen	17	4	0–4
			Average				13		
Battle wagons and crew	Battle Wagons	–	Average	Undrilled	Crossbow	Heavy Weapon	23	2–4	4–8

Hussite War Wagon, by Angus McBride. Taken from Men-at-Arms 409: The Hussite Wars 1419–36.

LATER HUNGARIAN

After the death of Albrecht of Habsburg, the Hungarian throne went to the Polish King Władysław III (1440–1444), passing over the claim of Albrecht's son Ladislaus V Posthumus (born after Albrecht's death) who did not ascend the throne until Władysław's defeat and death at the Battle of Varna against the Ottomans. In 1453 Ladislaus was also crowned king of Bohemia. János Hunyadi, Voivode of Transylvania, acted as regent for the child king in Hungary, George of Poděbrady in Bohemia, Ulrich of Celje in Austria.

János Hunyadi commanded the Hungarian forces in the war against the Ottoman Turks from 1441 until his death in 1456, using mainly mercenary forces, principally Bohemians. Between 1441 and 1443 he won several victories over the Turks. However, at Varna in 1444 the combined Hungarian-Polish army under King Władysław and Hunyadi was heavily defeated,

Hungarian Commander

Władysław being killed. The Hungarians, under Hunyadi, were defeated again at the Second Battle of Kosovo in 1448. In 1456, however, with his own well-armed forces and a large force of poorly armed mainly German crusaders, he decisively defeated the Turks at Belgrade, forcing them to lift the siege and retire. Disease broke out in the camp soon afterwards, however, resulting in Hunyadi's death.

Ladislaus died, aged 17, in 1457, possibly from poison, possibly of leukaemia. He was succeeded in Austria by his cousin Frederick V. Matthias Corvinus, son of the hero János Hunyadi, was elected King of Hungary in 1458 at the age of 15. George of Poděbrady was elected King of Bohemia.

Matthias Corvinus (1458–1490), with his "Black Army" of, once again, mainly Bohemian mercenaries, successfully resisted and retaliated against the Turks: In Bosnia (1463–1464), Southern Hungary (1475), Transylvania, Wallachia, Serbia and Bosnia (1479–1483). In 1467 a Hungarian invasion of Moldavia under Matthias was defeated by Stephen the Great at the Battle of Baia. In 1469, Matthias was crowned King of Bohemia, in Catholic opposition to the Hussite George of Poděbrady. By the Peace of Olomouc in 1479, Bohemia was partitioned between Matthias (who ruled Moravia, Silesia, and Lusatia) and George of Poděbrady's elected successor, Ladislaus II Jagiellon, son of King Casimir IV of Poland. Matthias also occupied half of modern Austria, claiming the title of Duke of Austria, and ruling from Vienna from 1485 until his death. He was succeeded as King of Hungary by Ladislaus Jagiellon, King of Bohemia, who ruled until his death in 1516.

This list covers Hungarian armies from 1441 to 1500.

TROOP NOTES

Classification of Szeklers presents some difficulty, so we have given a choice of interpretations.

LATER HUNGARIAN STARTER ARMY		
Commander-in-Chief	1	Field Commander
Sub-commanders	2	2 x Troop Commander
Hungarian nobles	2 BGs	Each comprising 4 bases of Hungarian nobles: Superior, Heavily Armoured, Undrilled Knights – Lancers, Swordsmen
Szeklers	2 BGs	Each comprising 4 bases of szeklers: Average, Protected, Undrilled Cavalry – Bow, Swordsmen
Hungarian horse archers	2 BGs	Each comprising 4 bases of Hungarian horse archers: Average, Unprotected, Undrilled Light Horse – Bow
Clipeati, armati and supporting archers	2 BGs	Each comprising 9 bases of Clipeati, armati and supporting archers: 6 Average, Protected, Drilled Heavy Foot – Defensive spearmen plus 3 Average, Unprotected, Drilled Light Foot – Bow
Handgunners	1 BG	6 bases of handgunners: Average, Protected, Drilled Light Foot – Firearm
Camp	1	Unfortified camp
Total	9 BGs	Camp, 24 mounted bases, 24 foot bases, 3 commanders

BUILDING A CUSTOMISED LIST USING OUR ARMY POINTS

Choose an army based on the maxima and minima in the list below. The following special instructions apply to this army:

- Commanders should be depicted as royal banderium, Hungarian nobles or mercenary men-at-arms.
- The minima marked * apply if any handgunners (other than those assumed to be making up part of war wagon crews) are used.
- Only one allied contingent can be used.

Handgunner

LATER HUNGARIAN

Territory Types: Agricultural, Hilly

C-in-C	Inspired Commander/Field Commander/Troop Commander					80/50/35	1	
Sub-commanders	Field Commander					50	0–2	
	Troop Commander					35	0–3	

Troop name	Troop Type				Capabilities		Points per base	Bases per BG	Total bases
	Type	Armour	Quality	Training	Shooting	Close Combat			
Core Troops									
Royal banderium	Knights	Heavily Armoured	Superior	Drilled	–	Lancers, Swordsmen	26	4	0–4
Hungarian nobles	Knights	Heavily Armoured	Superior	Undrilled	–	Lancers, Swordsmen	23	4–6	0–12
Mercenary men-at-arms	Knights	Heavily Armoured	Average	Drilled	–	Lancers, Swordsmen	21	4–6	0–12
Hungarian or other light horse archers	Light Horse	Unprotected	Average	Undrilled	Bow	–	8	4–6	6–12
Szeklers	Light Horse	Unprotected	Superior	Undrilled	Bow	Swordsmen	12	4–6	0–18
			Average				10		
	Light Horse	Unprotected	Superior	Undrilled	Bow	Light Spear, Swordsmen	13		
			Average				11		
	Cavalry	Unprotected	Superior	Undrilled	Bow	Swordsmen	12		
		Unprotected	Average				10		
		Protected	Superior				14		
		Protected	Average				11		
	Cavalry	Unprotected	Superior	Undrilled	Bow*	Light Spear, Swordsmen	12		
		Unprotected	Average				10		
		Protected	Superior				14		
		Protected	Average				11		
	Cavalry	Armoured	Superior	Undrilled	Bow*	Light Spear, Swordsmen	18	4–6	0–6
Clipeati and armati	Heavy Foot	Armoured	Average	Drilled	–	Defensive Spearmen	9	2/3 or all	*8–24
		Protected					7	6–12	
Supporting foot archers	Light Foot	Unprotected	Average	Drilled	Bow	–	5	1/3 or 0	
Crossbowmen	Light Foot	Unprotected	Average	Drilled	Crossbow	–	5	6–8	0–12
Handgunners	Light Foot	Unprotected	Average	Drilled	Firearm	–	4	*6–12	*6–18
		Protected					5		
Optional Troops									
Polish men-at-arms	Knights	Heavily Armoured	Superior	Undrilled	–	Lancers, Swordsmen	23	4	0–4
Tatars	Light Horse	Unprotected	Average	Undrilled	Bow	Swordsmen	10	4–6	0–6
	Cavalry	Unprotected	Average	Undrilled	Bow	Swordsmen	10		
		Protected					11		
Serbian hussars	Light Horse	Unprotected	Average	Undrilled	–	Lancers, Swordsmen	8	4–6	0–8
Separately deployed foot archers	Medium Foot	Unprotected	Average	Undrilled	Bow	–	5	6–8	0–12
			Poor				3		
	Light Foot	Unprotected	Average	Undrilled	Bow	–	5	6–8	
			Poor				3		
Peasants	Mob	Unprotected	Poor	Undrilled	–	–	2	8–12	0–12
Light guns	Light Artillery	–	Average	Undrilled	Light Artillery	–	15	2	0–2
Heavy guns	Heavy Artillery	–	Average	Undrilled	Heavy Artillery	–	20	2	0–2
War Wagons	Battle Wagons	–	Average	Undrilled	Crossbow	Heavy Weapon	23	2–4	0–6
Fortified camp							24		0–1
Allies									
Moldavian allies – Moldavian or Wallachian									
Polish allies (Only before 1444) – Later Polish									
Serbian allies (Only before 1447) – Later Serbian									
Wallachian allies – Moldavian or Wallachian									

LATER HUNGARIAN ALLIES

Allied commander	Field Commander/Troop Commander						40/25		1
Troop name	**Troop Type**				**Capabilities**		**Points per base**	**Bases per BG**	**Total bases**
	Type	Armour	Quality	Training	Shooting	Close Combat			
Hungarian nobles	Knights	Heavily Armoured	Superior	Undrilled	–	Lancers, Swordsmen	23	4–6	4–8
Mercenary men-at-arms	Knights	Heavily Armoured	Average	Drilled	–	Lancers, Swordsmen	21	4–6	
Hungarian or other light horse archers	Light Horse	Unprotected	Average	Undrilled	Bow	–	8	4	0–4
Szeklers	Light Horse	Unprotected	Superior	Undrilled	Bow	Swordsmen	12		
			Average				10		
	Light Horse	Unprotected	Superior	Undrilled	Bow	Light Spear, Swordsmen	13		
			Average				11		
	Cavalry	Unprotected	Superior	Undrilled	Bow	Swordsmen	12	4–6	0–6
		Unprotected	Average				10		4–10
		Protected	Superior				14		
		Protected	Average				11		
	Cavalry	Unprotected	Superior	Undrilled	Bow*	Light Spear, Swordsmen	12		
		Unprotected	Average				10		
		Protected	Superior				14		
		Protected	Average				11		
Clipeati and armati	Heavy Foot	Armoured	Average	Drilled	–	Defensive Spearmen	9	2/3 or all	*6–9
		Protected					7		
Supporting foot archers	Light Foot	Unprotected	Average	Drilled	Bow	–	5	1/3 or 0	6–9
Crossbowmen	Light Foot	Unprotected	Average	Drilled	Crossbow	–	5	4–6	*4–6
Handgunners	Light Foot	Unprotected	Average	Drilled	Firearm	–	4	4–6	
		Protected					5		

APPENDIX 1 – USING THE LISTS

To give balanced games, armies can be selected using the points system. The more effective the troops, the more each base costs in points. The maximum points for an army will usually be set at between 600 and 800 points for a singles game for 2 to 4 hours play. We recommend 800 points for 15mm singles tournament games (650 points for 25mm) and 1000 points for 15mm doubles games.

The army lists specify which troops can be used in a particular army. No other troops can be used. The number of bases of each type in the army must conform to the specified minima and maxima. Troops that have restrictions on when they can be used cannot be used with troops with a conflicting restriction. For example, troops that can only be used "before 1350" cannot be used with troops that can only be used "from 1350". All special instructions applying to an army list must be adhered to. They also apply to allied contingents supplied by the army.

All armies must have a C-in-C and at least one other commander. No army can have more than 4 commanders in total, including C-in-C, sub-commanders and allied commanders.

All armies must have a supply camp. This is free unless fortified. A fortified camp can only be used if specified in the army list. Field fortifications and portable defences can only be used if specified in the army list.

Allied contingents can only be used if specified in the army list. Most allied contingents have their own allied contingent list, to which they must conform unless the main army's list specifies otherwise.

BATTLE GROUPS

All troops are organized into battle groups. Commanders, supply camps and field fortifications are not troops and are not assigned to battle groups. Portable defences are not troops, but are assigned to specific battle groups.

Battle groups must obey the following restrictions:

- The number of bases in a battle group must correspond to the range specified in the army list.
- Each battle group must initially comprise an even number of bases. The only exception to this rule is that battle groups whose army list specifies them as 2/3 of one type and 1/3 of another, can comprise 9 bases if this is within the battle group size range specified by the list.
- A battle group can only include troops from one line in a list, unless the list specifies a mixed formation by specifying fractions of the battle group to be of types from two lines.

e.g. 2/3 spearmen, 1/3 archers.

- All troops in a battle group must be of the same quality and training. When a choice of quality or training is given in a list, this allows battle groups to differ from each other. It does not permit variety within a battle group.
- Unless specifically stated otherwise in an army list, all troops in a battle group must be of the same armour class. When a choice of armour class is given in a list, this allows battle groups to differ from each other. It does not permit variety within a battle group.

EXAMPLE LIST

Here is a section of an actual army list, which will help us to explain the basics and some special features. The list specifies the following items for each historical type included in the army:

- Troop Type - comprising Type, Armour, Quality and Training.
- Capabilities – comprising Shooting and Close Combat capabilities.
- Points cost per base.
- Minimum and maximum number of bases in each battle group.
- Minimum and maximum number of bases in the army.

Troop name	Troop Type				Capabilities		Points per base	Bases per BG	Total bases
	Type	Armour	Quality	Training	Shooting	Close Combat			
Feudal nobles and strzelcy	Knights	Heavily Armoured	Superior	Undrilled	–	Lancers, Swordsmen	23	1/2 or all	6–24
	Cavalry	Armoured	Superior	Undrilled	Crossbow	Swordsmen	17	1/2 or 0	0–24
		Protected					13		
Separately deployed strzelcy	Cavalry	Armoured	Average	Undrilled	Crossbow	Swordsmen	13	4–6	0–16
		Protected					10		
Lithuanian cavalry	Light Horse	Unprotected	Average	Undrilled	Bow	Light Spear, Swordsmen	11	4–6	0–6 before 1386, 0–24 from 1386
	Cavalry	Unprotected	Average	Undrilled	Bow*	Light Spear, Swordsmen	10		
		Protected					11		
Town militia crossbowmen and pavisiers	Heavy Foot	Protected	Average	Drilled	–	Defensive Spearmen	7	1/2	0–12
	Medium Foot	Protected	Average	Drilled	Crossbow	–	7	1/2	

The "4–6" for Bases per BG spans the Feudal nobles rows, and "12–48" spans the Total bases for Feudal nobles.

SPECIAL FEATURES:

- Battle groups of feudal nobles and strzelcy can be represented either all as Knights (the strzelcy being assumed to fill in the back ranks of each Knights base), or as half Knights, half Cavalry (representing the same thing in a deeper formation with a higher proportion of strzelcy). Srzelcy can also be deployed in separate all-Cavalry battle groups. When in mixed battle groups the morale of the strzelcy is assumed to be stiffened by the nobles, so they are graded as of Superior quality. When on their own they are graded as of Average quality. Strzelcy Cavalry can be graded as Armoured or Protected — the list gives the points cost for each. All strzelcy Cavalry in a battle group must be graded the same. Each battle group must contain either 4 or 6 bases. The army must include at least 6 bases of Knights, and at least 12 total bases of feudal nobles and strzelcy. It cannot include more than 24 bases of Knights, more than 24 bases of strzelcy Cavalry in mixed battle groups, or more than 16 bases of strzelcy Cavalry in separate battle groups. The total number of feudal nobles and strzelcy in the army cannot exceed 48 bases.

- Lithuanian cavalry can either be fielded as Unprotected Light Horse, Bow, Light Spear, Swordsmen, or as Unprotected or Protected Cavalry, Bow*, Light Spear, Swordsmen. Each battle group must contain either 4 or 6 bases. All the bases in a battle group must be graded the same. The maximum total number of bases of Lithuanian cavalry in the army is 6 before 1386 AD, 24 thereafter.

- Town militia crossbowmen and pavisiers must be organized into battle groups of 6 bases, 3 Heavy Foot with Defensive Spearmen capability and 3 Medium Foot with Crossbow capability. The maximum total number of bases in the army is 12.

APPENDIX 2 – THEMED TOURNAMENTS

A tournament based on the "Rise of the Ottomans" theme can include any of the armies listed in this book.

It can also include the following armies from our other army list books. These can only use options permitted between 1300 and 1500 AD inclusive:

SWORDS AND SCIMITARS

Mamluk Egyptian

Medieval Cypriot

STORM OF ARROWS

Venetians outside Italy (Italian Condotta)

Note: Some of the army lists referenced in this book are planned either to be included in future *Field of Glory* Companions or as free downloads from the *Field of Glory* website. We have included them in these lists for the sake of historical accuracy.

Visit www.fieldofglory.com to keep up-to-date with the latest Companion and army list releases.

INDEX